Environmental Chemistry

Alan Winfield

Series editor
Fred Webber

CAMBRIDGE
UNIVERSITY PRESS

Published by the Press Syndicate of the University of Cambridge
The Pitt Building, Trumpington Street, Cambridge CB2 1RP
40 West 20th Street, New York, NY 10011-4211, USA
10 Stamford Road, Oakleigh, Melbourne 3166, Australia

First published 1995

Printed in Great Britain at the University Press, Cambridge

A catalogue record for this book is available from the British Library

ISBN 0 521 42156 X paperback

Designed and produced by Gecko Ltd, Bicester, Oxon

This book is one of a series produced to support
individual modules within the Cambridge Modular
Sciences scheme. Teachers should note that written
examinations will be set on the content of each module as
defined in the syllabus. This book is the author's
interpretation of the module.

Front cover photograph: Limestone pavement showing clints and
grykes in the Yorkshire Dales, England; Martyn Chillmaid/Oxford
Scientific Films

Contents

Introduction

Like all chemical systems the chemistry of our wider environment is a question of balance, that of mutually inter-related systems whose balance depends on each other. If we destroy this balance by our thoughtless interference, the consequences can have far-reaching effects. In this book we shall study the relationships between the chemical systems that occur naturally on our Earth, and the effects of human activity upon these systems. For the purposes of this study the environment has been divided into the atmosphere (the air), the hydrosphere (the water in rivers and oceans) and the lithosphere (the soil and rock of the Earth).

Acknowledgements

1, Images Colour Library; 2, Lionel Moss/Life File; 8*l*, Garden/Wildlife Matters Photo Library; 8*c*, Steve Turner/Oxford Scientific Films; 8*r*, Steve Kaufman/Bruce Coleman Ltd; 9*t*, *table 2.1* from Warren Springs Laboratory, on behalf of the DOE, first published in the *Digest of Environmental Protection and Water Statistics*, **16**, 1994: Crown copyright is reproduced with the permission of the Controller of HMSO; 9*b*, 14*t*, 18*t*, 26*c*, 41, courtesy of Dr J. E. Fergusson, University of Canterbury, New Zealand; 14, V. Miles/ Environmental Picture Library; 16*l*, Andy Tickle/ Greenpeace/Environmental Picture Library; 16*r*, 46, Mark N. Boulton/Bruce Coleman Ltd; 17, Hulton Deutsch Collection; 18*b*, 25*b*, 65*b*, Bond, R. G., and Straub, C. P., *Handbook of Environmental Control*, **1**, Chemical Rubber Co. Press, Cleveland, USA; 21*b*, Logan, J. R., *J. Geophys. Res.*, **88**, 10785; 24, *figure 2.3* reproduced by permission from Harrison, R. M. (ed.), *Understanding Our Environment*, Royal Society of Chemistry, Cambridge, 1992; 26, courtesy of Johnson Matthey Catalytic Systems Division; 28, NASA GSFC/Science Photo Library; 31, Jane Burton/Bruce Coleman Ltd; 32, Michael Brooke; 36, 51, 59*t*, Ben Osborne/Oxford Scientific Films; 40, Bernard Nimtsch/Greenpeace/ Environmental Picture Library; 44, Nick Hawkes/ Echoscene; 48, ©Anglian Water Authority/photo by Sealand Aerial Photography; 49*b* , *table 4.2* reproduced by permission from Phillips, P. and Pickering, P., *School Science Review*, The Association for Science Education, 1991; 52*t*, 52*c*, 52*bl*, Andrew Lambert; 52*br*, GeoScience Features Picture Library; 55*l*, The Natural History Museum, London; 55*r*, Dave Thompson/Life File; 57, Nigel Cattlin/Holt Studios International; 59*b*, Fitzpatrick, E. A., *Soil Science*, Longman Group Limited, 1974; 61*l*, Martyn Chillmaid/Oxford Scientific Films; 61*r*, Ian Richards/Life File; 64, 68, Tick Ahearn; 66*t*, Amanda Gazidis/Greenpeace/ Environmental Picture Library; 66*b*, G. Burns/ Environmental Picture Library

The atmosphere

1 describe the structure of the atmosphere in terms of troposphere, stratosphere, mesosphere and thermosphere;

2 describe the composition and temperature variations of each of the four main regions of the atmosphere;

3 explain some of the important reactions which take place in the troposphere;

4 explain the absorption of ultraviolet radiation in the stratosphere;

5 explain the cycle of ozone formation and destruction;

6 explain the absorption of ultraviolet radiation in the mesosphere and thermosphere.

The Earth's atmosphere is essential for life *(figure 1.1)*. Oxygen is required for respiration by animals and plants, carbon dioxide is needed for photosynthesis, nitrogen is used for making proteins, and ozone protects us from the Sun's harmful rays.

It has not always been this way. Five billion (5 000 000 000) years ago the atmosphere consisted primarily of water vapour, carbon dioxide and nitrogen. At this time the Earth was cooling, and heavy rains washed out most of the carbon dioxide. Around three billion years ago simple cells evolved into organisms capable of photosynthesis. This produced oxygen, which has built up to create the atmosphere as we know it today. Part of the oxygen was changed into ozone by the Sun's radiation. Thus the conditions were created for the huge diversity of life now present on the Earth's surface.

The atmosphere extends roughly 2000 km above the Earth's surface. To study it, we divide it into four regions. These are the troposphere, the stratosphere, the mesosphere and the thermosphere. The atmosphere becomes less dense the higher you go.

The troposphere

The troposphere contains 90% of the molecules in the atmosphere and extends from the Earth's surface up to between 10 km and 16 km, depending on the latitude. The temperature at the top of the layer is around 200 K. Mixing of different chemicals in this region is fast and this layer contains our familiar weather patterns. The dry atmosphere at sea level contains 78.09% nitrogen, 20.94% oxygen, 0.93% argon, 0.03% carbon dioxide and traces of other gases. Important chemical reactions that take place in the troposphere include photosynthesis and nitrogen fixation.

Photosynthesis

During photosynthesis green plants convert carbon dioxide and water into oxygen and sugars such as glucose:

$$6CO_2(g) + 6H_2O(l) \xrightarrow[\text{chlorophyll}]{\text{sunlight } hf} C_6H_{12}O_6(aq) + 6O_2(g);$$
$$\Delta H = +2820 \text{ kJ} \quad (1.1)$$

(The energy of radiation is given by the equation $E = hf$, where E = energy, h = Planck's constant and f = frequency of radiation, so the symbol hf is used for radiation in chemical equations.)

● *Figure 1.1*

Photosynthesis is one of the most important processes in the world as it harnesses the energy of the Sun, and some of this energy may be transformed into the chemical energy of fossil fuels. The energy of these is in turn converted to heat energy when the fuels are combusted, and thence to electrical energy via the turbines of a power station, for use in homes, offices, industry and transport. Photosynthesis is essential for the formation of agricultural products such as food, oils, forestry products, and organic and inorganic chemicals *(figure 1.2)*.

The solar energy collectors in plants are mainly green chlorophylls, which are complex nitrogen-based organic chemicals with magnesium at their centre. Most solar energy is collected at wavelengths of around 660–680 nm (red light) and 425 nm (blue). Energy with a wavelength of around 430 nm is also absorbed, to protect the plant from radiation damage and for use in photosynthesis. This absorption of light leaves the plant looking green.

A more detailed mechanism for *reaction 1.1* can be explained in the following terms.

- Solar energy is used in the so-called 'light' reaction to decompose water to provide electrons:

$$2H_2O(l) \xrightarrow{\text{sunlight } hf} O_2(g) + 4H^+(aq) + 4e^- \quad (1.2)$$

- The conversion of carbon dioxide into carbohydrates is a 'dark' reaction not requiring solar energy:

$$nCO_2(g) + 4nH^+(aq) + 4ne^- \longrightarrow n[CH_2O](aq) + nH_2O(l) \quad (1.3)$$
$$\underset{\text{carbohydrates}}{}$$

- Respiration in animals and plants involves the oxidation of these carbohydrates, the release of their stored energy and the return of carbon dioxide to the atmosphere:

$$n[CH_2O](aq) + nO_2(g) \longrightarrow nCO_2(g) + nH_2O(l) \quad (1.4)$$
$$\underset{\text{carbohydrate}}{}$$

The destruction of rainforest *(figure 1.3)* may disturb this balance of reactions, by removing substantial numbers of plants from the equation.

SAQ 1.1

Which areas of the visible spectrum does chlorophyll

a absorb

b reflect?

SAQ 1.2

Suggest how farmers can modify the conditions in a greenhouse to produce lettuces throughout the year.

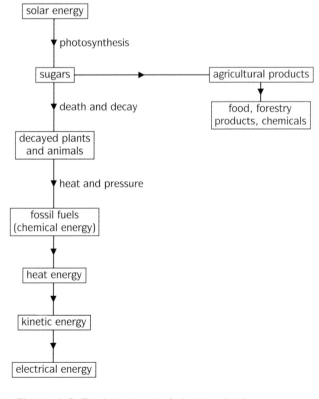

● *Figure 1.2* The importance of photosynthesis.

● *Figure 1.3* Rainforest in Kota Kinabalu National Park, Malaysia. The warm and humid conditions in tropical rainforests encourage rapid photosynthesis.

The carbon cycle

The concentration of carbon dioxide in the troposphere depends on the various processes involved in the carbon cycle *(figure 1.4)*. Carbon dioxide is removed from the atmosphere in photosynthesis:

$$nCO_2(g) + nH_2O(l) \longrightarrow n[CH_2O](aq) + nO_2(g) \qquad (1.5)$$

and returned to the atmosphere by respiration in plants and animals:

$$n[CH_2O](aq) + nO_2(g) \longrightarrow nCO_2(g) + nH_2O(l) \qquad (1.6)$$

Atmospheric carbon dioxide is also in dynamic equilibrium with carbon dioxide dissolved in surface water. Dynamic equilibrium (see chapter 2, page 12) means that the concentrations of gaseous and aqueous (dissolved) carbon dioxide remain constant even though there is a constant movement of individual molecules between the atmosphere and surface water:

$$CO_2(g) \rightleftharpoons CO_2(aq) \qquad (1.7)$$

Cold surface water found in oceans at high latitudes, for example in the Norwegian Sea and off southern Greenland, has a higher density than warmer water and so this surface water sinks rapidly to great depths, taking dissolved carbon dioxide with it. When a chemical species is removed from the atmosphere by some means like this, the place where it ends up is called an **atmospheric sink**. Hence the cold oceans are an important sink for the removal of atmospheric carbon dioxide.

Dissolved carbon dioxide reacts further with water and establishes dynamic equilibria that are discussed in more detail in chapter 3:

$$CO_2(aq) + H_2O(l) \rightleftharpoons H^+(aq) + HCO_3^-(aq)$$
$$\rightleftharpoons 2H^+(aq) + CO_3^{2-}(aq) \qquad (1.8)$$

In general, the concentrations of carbon are in balance in the different sections of the cycle, but variations in the carbon dioxide

content of the air do occur: there is more carbon dioxide at night and in the winter. Carbon dioxide concentration is increased by the combustion of fossil fuels and the removal of large areas of tropical rainforest, where photosynthesis is particularly rapid.

SAQ 1.3
Predict how the destruction of large tracts of tropical rainforest may affect the atmosphere.

Nitrogen fixation

At the start of this chapter we saw that about 78% of the troposphere is nitrogen gas. This nitrogen becomes part of biological matter, almost entirely by nitrogen fixation. The fixation of nitrogen is the conversion of atmospheric nitrogen into a water-soluble form which plants can take up through their roots.

Nitrogen gas, N_2, is very stable because it contains a strong triple bond, $N\equiv N$, of dissociation energy $+945\,kJ\,mol^{-1}$. The nitrogen molecule has an ionisation energy of $1505\,kJ\,mol^{-1}$ for the process

$$N_2(g) \longrightarrow N_2^+(g) + e^-$$

This energy is almost the same as that of the noble gas argon so nitrogen fixation does not take place easily. Over half the annual fixation of nitrogen in the world occurs naturally. The remainder is brought about by fertiliser production and combustion.

Biological fixation occurs in soils using nitrogenase enzymes. Enzymes are biological catalysts that speed up the chemical reactions in living systems. They are

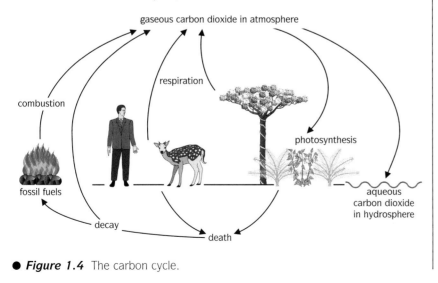

gaseous carbon dioxide in atmosphere

respiration

combustion

photosynthesis

fossil fuels

aqueous carbon dioxide in hydrosphere

decay

death

● *Figure 1.4* The carbon cycle.

very specific in their action and normally only work on one particular stage of a reaction. Enzymes are usually named after the substance they act upon (in this case nitrogen) plus '-ase'. Nitrogenase enzymes occur in such bacteria as *Clostridium* and *Azotobacter*, or in the root nodules of plants such as legumes (peas, clover).

The direct value of nitrogen fixation to humans is in the growth of crops. Nitrogen is essential for the formation of amino acids and proteins. If biological nitrogen fixation is insufficient for crop needs, it is necessary to add nitrogen fertilisers at certain times of the year.

Nitrogenase enzymes reduce nitrogen to ammonia. The mechanism of this reaction is very complex, involving molybdenum and iron protein molecules of very high relative molecular mass ($M_r \sim 222\,000$). Some ammonia is taken into plants through the root systems and is used in the biosynthesis of amino acids, for example:

$$2NH_3(aq) + 2H_2O(l) + 4CO_2(g)$$
$$\longrightarrow 2NH_2CH_2COOH(aq) + 3O_2(g) \quad (1.9)$$
$$\text{aminoethanoic acid}$$

Nitrification reactions in the soil oxidise the ammonia to nitrite, NO_2^-, then nitrate, NO_3^-:

$$2NH_3(aq) + 3O_2(g)$$
$$\longrightarrow 2H^+(aq) + 2NO_2^-(aq) + 2H_2O(l) \quad (1.10)$$

$$2NO_2^-(aq) + O_2(g) \longrightarrow 2NO_3^-(aq) \quad (1.11)$$

These reactions are also catalysed by bacterial enzymes.

Some 4% of nitrogen is fixed by the action of lightning. Nitrogen and oxygen from the atmosphere combine directly to form nitrogen monoxide:

$$N_2(g) + O_2(g) \xrightarrow{\text{lightning}} 2NO(g) \quad (1.12)$$

The nitrogen monoxide formed is only slowly oxidised to nitrogen dioxide at the low concentrations that exist in the atmosphere. Oxidation is much more rapid in the presence of the secondary pollutant, ozone (page 23).

The quantities of nitrogen oxides in the atmosphere are decreased by reacting with water to form very dilute nitric acid:

$$3NO_2(g) + H_2O(l) \longrightarrow 2HNO_3(aq) + NO(g) \quad (1.13)$$

(The precise mechanism involves reaction with hydroxyl radicals, $NO_2 + \cdot OH \rightarrow HNO_3$.)

Much of the nitrogen that has been fixed is returned to the atmosphere when nitrates and nitrites are broken down in the soil. This is also catalysed by bacterial enzymes and the process is called **denitrification**. For example:

$$4NO_3^-(aq) + 2H_2O(l)$$
$$\longrightarrow 2N_2(g) + 5O_2(g) + 4OH^-(aq) \quad (1.14)$$

All these reactions are linked in the **nitrogen cycle** (*figure 1.5*).

The need for the addition of nitrogenous fertilisers has already been mentioned. There is concern that the increased use of nitrogenous fertilisers may be leading to an increase of dinitrogen oxide, N_2O, in the atmosphere, via the soil denitrification process:

$$6NO_3^-(aq) + C_6H_{12}O_6(aq)$$
$$\text{glucose (from plants)}$$
$$\longrightarrow 6CO_2(g) + 3H_2O(l)$$
$$+ 6OH^-(aq) + 3N_2O(g) \quad (1.15)$$

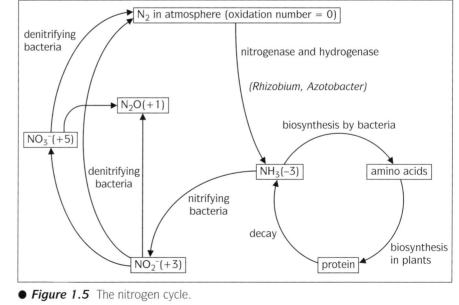

● *Figure 1.5* The nitrogen cycle.

Dinitrogen oxide is unreactive in the troposphere, but may rise into the stratosphere, where it can influence ozone levels.

SAQ 1.4

Explain why lack of nitrogen causes stunted growth in plants. Why does it cause leaves to turn yellow?

The stratosphere

The stratosphere extends from 10–16 km to 60 km above the Earth's surface. The temperature of the stratosphere rises from just above 200 K at 12 km to 290 K at 60 km (*figure 1.6*).

The stratosphere contains nitrogen, oxygen, ozone and some water vapour. These chemical species are active because radiation acts upon them, producing chemical change. This sort of change is called **photochemistry**.

The radiation principally responsible for change in the stratosphere is ultraviolet of longer wavelengths. For example, the production of ozone is brought about by ultraviolet radiation of wavelengths between 190 nm and 242 nm.

Ozone is a form of oxygen with three oxygen atoms. It is produced in the stratosphere by the following photochemical reactions:

$$O_2(g) \xrightarrow{hf} O(g) + O^*(g) \qquad (1.16)$$

$$O^*(g) + O_2(g) + M(g) \longrightarrow O_3(g) + M^*(g);$$
$$\text{ozone}$$
$$\Delta H = -100 \, kJ \, mol^{-1} \qquad (1.17)$$

M is a third chemical species required to take away excess energy. In the atmosphere this is usually molecular nitrogen and oxygen. An asterisk (*) is used to indicate energy-rich atoms or molecules. Thus in *reaction 1.16* solar radiation produces energy-rich, sometimes called 'excited', oxygen atoms. In *reaction 1.17* M carries off excess energy as M^*.

The ozone produced absorbs ultraviolet radiation of wavelengths less than 340 nm in two reactions that re-form diatomic oxygen:

$$O_3(g) \xrightarrow{hf} O_2(g) + O(g) \qquad (1.18)$$

followed by

$$O_3(g) + O(g) \longrightarrow 2O_2(g);$$
$$\Delta H = -390 \, kJ \, mol^{-1} \qquad (1.19)$$

Figure 1.6 shows that below the stratosphere there is a decrease in the temperature of the atmosphere as height above the Earth's surface increases, up to approximately 15 km. After this the temperature increases with height. You can see that *reactions 1.17* and *1.19* produce a considerable amount of heat and this causes the increase in temperature that occurs with an increase in height in the stratosphere (the reactions are more likely to occur as height increases, because there is more ultraviolet radiation).

The change from decreasing temperature to increasing temperature is a **temperature inversion**, and the height at which this change occurs is called the **tropopause**.

It is the absorption of ultraviolet radiation in the stratosphere which prevents most radiation of wavelengths less than 320 nm from reaching the Earth. In this way, plants and animals are protected from this radiation.

There are other reactions which remove ozone. The most important of these are

● *Figure 1.6* The variation of temperature with height from the Earth's surface.

free-radical reactions *(box 1A)* with oxides of nitrogen, which occur at a height of roughly 25 km:

$$NO{\cdot}(g) + O_3(g) \longrightarrow NO_2{\cdot}(g) + O_2(g);$$
$$\Delta H = -200 \, kJ \, mol^{-1} \qquad (1.20)$$

$$NO_2{\cdot}(g) + O(g) \longrightarrow NO{\cdot}(g) + O_2(g);$$
$$\Delta H = -192 \, kJ \, mol^{-1} \qquad (1.21)$$

$$NO_2{\cdot}(g) \xrightarrow{hf} NO{\cdot}(g) + O(g) \qquad (1.22)$$

Note that the oxygen atom is recycled.

Box 1A Free-radical reactions

Reactions in the upper atmosphere (stratosphere, mesosphere and thermosphere) are mainly free-radical reactions initiated by the strong ultraviolet radiation provided by the Sun (see also chapter 2). **Free radicals** are reactive atoms or molecules with an unpaired electron. The reactions are chain processes that proceed by three stages. (All the reactions discussed in this box occur in the gaseous state.)

In the first stage, free radicals are produced by the action of ultraviolet radiation. This is called the **chain initiation** stage. Initiation reactions in the upper atmosphere are:

$$O_2 \xrightarrow{hf} O + O^* \text{ (O* represents energy-rich oxygen atom)}$$

$$O_3 \xrightarrow{hf} O_2 + O^*$$

$$O^* + H_2O \xrightarrow{hf} 2{\cdot}OH$$

$$O^* + CH_4 \xrightarrow{hf} {\cdot}CH_3 + {\cdot}OH$$

Once free radicals have been produced they can react with other molecules or atoms to produce further free radicals, and a chain reaction is produced. This is known as the **chain propagation** stage. Propagation reactions are:

$${\cdot}OH + O_3 \longrightarrow HO_2{\cdot} + O_2$$

$$HO_2{\cdot} + O \longrightarrow {\cdot}OH + O_2$$

$${\cdot}OH + O \longrightarrow O_2 + H{\cdot}$$

$$H{\cdot} + O_3 \longrightarrow {\cdot}OH + O_2$$

Collision of free radicals with each other removes these radicals. This is the **chain termination** stage. Termination reactions are:

$$NO_2{\cdot} + {\cdot}OH \longrightarrow HNO_3$$

$$HO_2{\cdot} + HO_2{\cdot} \longrightarrow H_2O_2 + O_2$$

The oxides of nitrogen used in *reactions 1.20* to *1.22* enter the atmosphere from biological activity (see page 20) and fossil fuel combustion.

Hydroxyl radicals, ·OH, are also involved in the removal of ozone. They are formed by the reaction of energy-rich oxygen atoms (from photolysis reactions) with water vapour:

$$O^*(g) + H_2O(g) \longrightarrow 2{\cdot}OH(g) \qquad (1.23)$$

These hydroxyl radicals can react with oxygen atoms in a chain reaction which produces more hydroxyl radicals:

$${\cdot}OH(g) + O(g) \longrightarrow O_2(g) + H{\cdot}(g);$$
$$\Delta H = -64 \, kJ \, mol^{-1} \qquad (1.24)$$

$$H{\cdot}(g) + O_3(g) \longrightarrow {\cdot}OH(g) + O_2(g);$$
$$\Delta H = -326 \, kJ \, mol^{-1} \qquad (1.25)$$

Above 45 km these reactions play an important role in the removal of ozone (see page 27).

SAQ 1.5

Explain why temperature increases with height in the stratosphere.

SAQ 1.6

State the reactions which **a** produce and **b** remove ozone in the stratosphere.

The mesosphere and the thermosphere

The next two regions of the atmosphere are the mesosphere and the thermosphere. The mesosphere extends from a height of approximately 60 km above the Earth's surface to about 90 km (where the thermosphere starts). In the mesosphere the temperature falls as the height increases, down to a minimum of 200 K. The thermosphere is the outermost region of the atmosphere. A temperature inversion occurs at a height of around 90 km. From this point on, the temperature rises from 200 K at 90 km to 1300 K in the outer regions, which are 700–800 km from the surface of the Earth *(figure 1.6)*. This temperature rise is produced by a two-stage process. First, photo-chemical reactions occur, such as:

$$O_2(g) \xrightarrow{hf} O(g) + O(g) \qquad (1.26)$$

Reactions such as this absorb radiation in the far ultraviolet, with a wavelength range of 135–176 nm. Second, reactions such as *1.17* and *1.19* occur, which produce heat.

Ions are produced in the lower layers of the thermosphere, so this region is sometimes called the **ionosphere**. The main ionic species are O_2^+, O^+, and NO^+. The electrical charge associated with these ions causes the ionosphere to reflect radio waves.

SAQ 1.7

Explain why ultraviolet radiation is absorbed in the thermosphere.

Residence time

The length of time a particular chemical is present in a given reservoir, for instance the atmosphere, is related to the rate of input of the chemical into the atmosphere from its sources and the rate of removal to various sinks. Think of a bath filling up with water. When the bath is full, if it is at equilibrium, then the rate of inflow from the tap is equal to the rate of outflow through the overflow (and possibly over the sides!). The tap is the source, the overflow is the sink and the bath is the reservoir. All non-permanent chemical species have sources, which put them into the atmosphere, and sinks, which remove them, for example the oceans. Once molecules of a chemical species are in the atmosphere, the length of time they remain is expressed by the residence time. This is the average time that molecules of the given species spend in the atmosphere.

The **residence time** (or lifetime) is given by the concentration of the given chemical species in the atmosphere divided by the rate of removal:

$$\text{residence time (lifetime) } T = \frac{\text{concentration of given species}}{\text{rate of removal}}$$

Some residence times are given in *table 2.2*.

SUMMARY

- The atmosphere may be divided into four regions: troposphere, stratosphere, mesosphere and thermosphere.
- Important reactions in the troposphere are photosynthesis and nitrogen fixation.
- The concentration of carbon dioxide in the atmosphere depends on photosynthesis, respiration and the amount of carbon dioxide dissolved in surface waters. These are linked in the carbon cycle.
- The circulation of nitrogen within the environment can be described by the nitrogen cycle.
- Ozone is important in the stratosphere as it absorbs ultraviolet radiation.
- Various dynamic chemical equilibria maintain the concentration of ozone in the stratosphere.
- Photochemical reactions in the thermosphere absorb in the far ultraviolet.
- Residence time reflects the relative rates at which substances are supplied to and removed from the atmosphere.

Questions

1 Name the four main regions of the Earth's atmosphere and state their approximate heights above the Earth's surface.
 Explain the variations in temperature with height (as shown in *figure 1.6*).

2 Explain the factors that affect the concentrations of nitrogen oxides in the unpolluted atmosphere.

Atmospheric pollutants

In December 1952 London was gripped by severe air pollution. In five days, more than 4000 people died from its effects. Most of these were elderly or sufferers from chronic respiratory disease. Incidents such as this and others like it (see page 17) have alerted us to the folly of using the atmosphere as some kind of gaseous dustbin.

Emissions of pollutants

Emissions into the atmosphere are in the form of either gases or particulate material (*figure 2.1*). The term **particulate material** refers to dusts and liquid droplets in which the particles can have a wide range of sizes (10^{-8}m to 10^{-4}m). Particulate material can also absorb gases.

Material emitted into the atmosphere is diluted with air and transported both vertically and horizontally. It also undergoes chemical and physical changes. Pollutants are either **primary**, in which case they are emitted directly into the atmosphere, or **secondary**, that is they have been formed indirectly by reactions in the atmosphere.

Some emissions accumulate in the atmosphere, for example carbon dioxide. Others that are unreactive in the troposphere escape into the stratosphere, where they participate in chemical reactions.

● *Figure 2.1* Both human and natural activities cause pollutants to be emitted into the atmosphere.

There are a whole host of air pollutants, the main ones being the oxides of carbon, sulphur dioxide, hydrogen sulphide, oxides of nitrogen and ozone. All of them have damaging effects on human and animal health, vegetation and building materials. Each pollutant will be discussed in turn, although the chemistry of their behaviour in the atmosphere is inter-related.

Table 2.1 gives figures for emissions of pollutants into the atmosphere arising from human activity in the United Kingdom for the year 1989. *Table 2.2* shows sources of emission on a global scale, both from natural sources and as a result of human activity.

Source	Black smoke	Sulphur dioxide	Nitrogen oxides	Carbon monoxide	Volatile organic compounds (excluding methane)
domestic	191	138	68	339	50
industrial	81	683	353	331	1435*
power stations	25	2640	769	47	12
refineries	2	109	35	1	107
road vehicles:					
petrol	15	22	848	6182	727
diesel	182	38	580	160	160
railways	–	3	32	12	8
gas leakage (during distribution)	–	–	–	–	34
other	4	88	157	31	18
total emission	500	3721	2842	7103	2551

* Includes evaporation of motor spirit during storage and distribution.

● *Table 2.1* Estimated UK emission of primary pollutants for 1989, measured in units of 10^3 tonnes

Material	Pollution sources	Natural sources	Time in atmosphere
carbon dioxide	combustion	biological decay	4 years
carbon monoxide	transport combustion	forest fires	1–4 months
hydrocarbons	transport combustion	biological processes	16 years
halogenocarbons	aerosols refrigerants	–	over 20 years
sulphur dioxide	combustion of fossil fuels	volcanoes	3–7 days
hydrogen sulphide	chemical industry	volcanoes biological processes	2 days
nitrogen oxides	combustion	biological processes	4 days
ammonia	waste treatment	biological decay	2 days
particulates	combustion	dust	varies

● *Table 2.2* The main gases emitted into the atmosphere and their sources

Name and describe the biological process which puts nitrogen oxides into the atmosphere.

Air pollution may be discussed either in terms of the chemical species emitted into the air or in terms of the sources of the pollutant. The chemistry involved includes photochemistry, acid–base chemistry and catalysis.

Photochemistry

Photochemical reactions play an important role in atmospheric pollution. These reactions are brought about by the action of electromagnetic radiation on matter.

The first step in such a reaction is the absorption of a photon of light by the reactant species to produce an electronically excited state A^*:

$$A \xrightarrow{hf} A^* \tag{2.1}$$

(h is the Planck constant and f the frequency of the radiation. The symbol hf represents one photon of light energy.)

A^* can then take part in further processes (M is an inert molecule which takes away the excess energy):

■ chemical change
  ● dissociation:
$$A^* \longrightarrow X + Y + \ldots \tag{2.2}$$
  ● reaction:
$$A^* + B \longrightarrow C + D + \ldots \tag{2.3}$$
  ● ionisation:
$$A^* \longrightarrow A^+ + e^- \tag{2.4}$$
■ A^* returned to ground state
  ● fluorescence:
$$A^* \longrightarrow A + hf \tag{2.5}$$
  ● phosphorescence:
$$A^* \longrightarrow A + hf' \tag{2.6}$$
  ● collisional deactivation:
$$A^* + M \longrightarrow A + M \tag{2.7}$$

The energy of visible and ultraviolet radiation is similar to that of the average chemical bond. Thus if a species absorbs photons from this region of the electromagnetic spectrum, bond dissociation can occur. For example:

$$\text{O–H (in water);} \qquad E = 464 \, \text{kJ} \, \text{mol}^{-1}$$

The speed of a wave (or photon) is related to its frequency and wavelength by:

$$\text{speed,} \ c = \text{frequency,} \ f \times \text{wavelength,} \ \lambda$$

The Planck equation expresses the relationship between a particular frequency of radiation and the energy associated with it:

$$\text{energy,} \ E = \text{constant,} \ h \times \text{frequency,} \ f$$

The constant h (the Planck constant) has a value of $6.63 \times 10^{-34} \, \text{J s}$.

Combining these two expressions gives:

$$\lambda = \frac{hc}{E}$$

For one mole of bonds we need to introduce the Avogadro constant L:

$$\lambda = \frac{Lhc}{E}$$

($L = 6.02 \times 10^{23} \, \text{mol}^{-1}$, speed of electromagnetic radiation, $c = 3.00 \times 10^8 \, \text{m s}^{-1}$).

Substituting the values given in the above expression, the wavelength of electromagnetic radiation required to split the O–H bond in water is given by

$$\lambda = \frac{Lhc}{E}$$

$$= \frac{6.02 \times 10^{23} \times 6.63 \times 10^{-34} \times 3.00 \times 10^8}{464 \times 10^3}$$

$$= 2.58 \times 10^{-7} \, \text{m}$$

$$= 258 \, \text{nm (in ultraviolet region)}$$

In the upper atmosphere, ultraviolet radiation with $\lambda < 290 \, \text{nm}$ is involved in photochemical reactions. In the troposphere, ultraviolet radiation with $\lambda < 400 \, \text{nm}$ may be involved (*figure 2.2*).

Calculate the wavelength of the radiation that will be absorbed by the O=O bond (bond energy = $497 \, \text{kJ} \, \text{mol}^{-1}$).

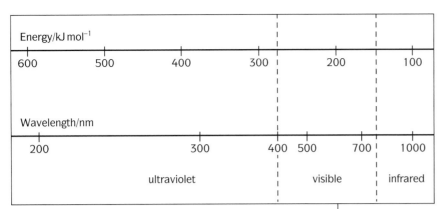

● *Figure 2.2* The relationship between energy and wavelength.

SAQ 2.3

Calculate the wavelength of the radiation that will be absorbed by the C—Cl bond (bond energy = $339\,kJ\,mol^{-1}$).

Temperature inversion

In the troposphere, air temperature normally decreases with height from the Earth's surface by about 1 °C for every 100 m of dry air. Sometimes the lowest layer of air is cooled by the ground beneath. This produces a temperature inversion as shown in *figure 2.3*. Ground level emissions then become trapped in the stable inversion layer. Lowered wind speed prevents the mixing of air levels and the lower polluted layer becomes stagnant. At low temperatures fog may form. This adds to the problem by reflecting the Sun's rays and preventing the warming of the lower layer. Pollutants prevent complete evaporation of the water droplets in fog, thus making the situation worse.

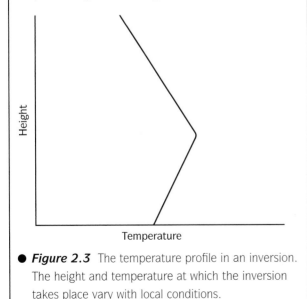

● *Figure 2.3* The temperature profile in an inversion. The height and temperature at which the inversion takes place vary with local conditions.

Oxides of carbon

Carbon monoxide and carbon dioxide are the pollutants produced in the largest quantities. The main sources are:

■ decomposition of organic material;
■ oxidation of methane;
■ combustion of fossil fuels.

The oxidation of carbon may be summarised as:

$$2C(s) + O_2(g) \longrightarrow 2CO(g);$$
$$\Delta H^{\ominus} = -220\,kJ \quad (2.8)$$

$$2CO(g) + O_2(g) \longrightarrow 2CO_2(g);$$
$$\Delta H^{\ominus} = -566\,kJ \quad (2.9)$$

The second reaction is slow because of the high activation energy to be overcome, due to the strong C≡O bond.

You may be surprised that more carbon monoxide is produced naturally, by the oxidation of methane from swamps and oxidation of organic material in the tropics, than is produced by the activities of man. The process is:

$$CH_4 + {\cdot}OH \longrightarrow {\cdot}CH_3 + H_2O \quad (2.10)$$

$${\cdot}CH_3 + O_2 + M \longrightarrow CH_3O_2{\cdot} + M \quad (2.11)$$

$$CH_3O_2{\cdot} + NO \longrightarrow CH_3O{\cdot} + NO_2 \quad (2.12)$$

$$CH_3O{\cdot} + O_2 \longrightarrow HCHO + HO_2{\cdot} \quad (2.13)$$

$$HCHO \xrightarrow{hf} H_2 + CO \quad (2.14)$$

All species are in the gaseous state. M is a third body on which the two species come together.

The emissions of carbon monoxide produced by human activity do not significantly add to the total worldwide, although there are local problems in urban areas.

Of the activities of humans, the fuels burnt for transport are the principal source of the oxides of carbon in the atmosphere. For carbon monoxide, the most significant source by far (56%) is petrol burnt in internal combustion engines. The burning of petrol accounts for 31% of carbon dioxide emissions. Most carbon monoxide is produced during idling and deceleration, because in these conditions the combustion mixture tends to be fuel rich. These stages are lowest in carbon dioxide emissions.

The ratio of $CO:CO_2$ in internal combustion engine emissions is determined by the position of balance of the reversible reaction:

$$CO_2 \rightleftharpoons CO + \tfrac{1}{2}O_2;$$
$$\Delta H = +1825\,\text{kJ}\,\text{mol}^{-1} \qquad (2.15)$$
(under the conditions of the internal combustion engine)

Chemical equilibrium

Most chemical reactions are in a position of balance. The reactants are not completely converted into products and the position of balance can be approached from either side. The intermediate position, at which both reactants and products are present and their concentration does not change at a given temperature, is known as the position of equilibrium. When this position is reached both the forward and backward reactions are taking place at equal rates. The reaction is said to be in **dynamic equilibrium.**

Thus in *reaction 2.15* carbon dioxide changes into carbon monoxide and oxygen. This is known as the forward reaction and is endothermic ($\Delta H = +1825\,\text{kJ}\,\text{mol}^{-1}$ under the conditions of the car engine). The reverse reaction, when carbon monoxide combines with oxygen to form carbon dioxide, is of course exothermic.

You can see that in *reaction 2.15* one mole of gas is converted into 1.5 moles of gas on the right-hand side of the equation, and conversely in going from the right to the left 1.5 moles change into one mole. **Avogadro's theory** states that 'Equal volumes of gases, under the same conditions of temperature and pressure, contain equal numbers of molecules.' Thus on going from right to left in *reaction 2.15*, 1.5 volumes of gas are reduced to 1 volume. If we want to reduce the amount of carbon monoxide in exhaust emissions, we need to increase the pressure to reduce 1.5 volumes of gas to 1 volume.

You have just seen that the reverse of *reaction 2.15*, $CO + \tfrac{1}{2}O_2 \longrightarrow CO_2$, is exothermic. Exothermic reactions are favoured by cooler surroundings. This enables the energy given out to be removed from the system.

These two points taken together tell us that to reduce the formation of carbon monoxide we need to lower the temperature, increase the pressure, and have a good supply of oxygen. Unfortunately these conditions increase the amounts of other pollutants, particularly oxides of nitrogen.

Carbon dioxide

Levels of carbon dioxide in the atmosphere have shown a steady increase since around 1870. There are seasonal variations in carbon dioxide concentration and in the northern hemisphere it peaks in April and is at its lowest in September and October. This seasonal variation is in the most part caused by photosynthesis in the mid-latitude forests. Destruction of the rainforests could have a serious effect in raising the levels of carbon dioxide in the atmosphere.

Climate depends on the global heat balance. A temperature change of 2–3 °C would have a pronounced effect on global and local climate. Of the energy which enters the Earth's atmosphere, 47% reaches the Earth's surface. Incoming energy has a maximum intensity at a wavelength of 483 nm. Energy re-emitted is in the infrared (2000–40 000 nm) with maximum intensity at 10 000 nm. Some of this infrared is absorbed by water vapour and carbon dioxide in the air and then re-emitted. The average temperature of the Earth's surface is maintained at 14 °C by the portion of this re-emitted radiation which is returned to Earth. If it was not for this re-emitted infrared radiation from water and carbon dioxide, the temperature of the Earth would be −20 °C to −40 °C at its surface. This method by which the Earth's surface is kept relatively warm is called the 'greenhouse effect', because it resembles the way in which greenhouses retain the Sun's warmth by internal reflection (*figure 2.4*).

There is increasing concern that rising levels of carbon dioxide in the atmosphere, together with other greenhouse gases discussed later, will lead to global warming with potentially disastrous climatic effects. As part of the International Geophysical Year in 1957, atmospheric monitoring stations were established at the South Pole and at Mauna Loa in

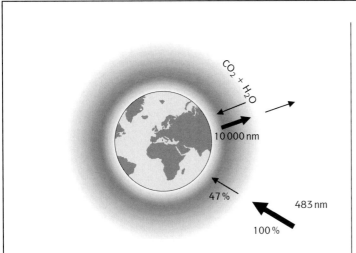

● *Figure 2.4* The 'greenhouse effect'. Some of the infrared radiation emitted by the Earth is absorbed by carbon dioxide, water and other 'greenhouse gases' in the atmosphere. Some of this radiation is re-emitted back to the Earth, keeping the Earth's surface relatively warm.

Hawaii. Figures for carbon dioxide concentration measured at Mauna Loa are given in *figure 2.5*.

Concentrations of pollutants in the atmosphere are measured in parts per million by volume, ppmv. This measure is frequently used where concentrations are very small. It could be explained as the number of particles of a given substance per million molecules of air; 350 ppmv corresponds to a concentration of 0.035%.

How can we possibly know what the carbon dioxide concentration was in 1850, just over 100

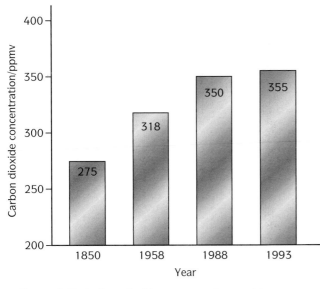

● *Figure 2.5* Carbon dioxide concentrations at Mauna Loa, Hawaii (see text for explanation of 1850 figure).

years before the station was set up? This 1850 figure has been obtained very ingeniously from measurements on bubbles of ancient air trapped in the ice sheets of Antarctica and Greenland. Successive measurements show an average annual rise of about 0.6 ppmv. As mentioned earlier there is a seasonal variation – of about 12 ppmv.

Most of the carbon dioxide put into the atmosphere artificially comes from the burning of fossil fuels. However, natural sources have led to substantial rises in carbon dioxide levels in the past, long before the appearance of artificial sources.

SAQ 2.4

In 1987 the fossil fuel equivalent of 6 billion tonnes of carbon was burnt. What mass of carbon dioxide will this produce? What assumption do you make in your calculation?

Carbon monoxide

The average, non-urban concentration of carbon monoxide has until recently remained relatively constant at 0.1–0.2 ppmv, in spite of the large quantities discharged into the atmosphere from motor vehicle emissions. There has been an upward trend in the UK since the mid-1980s. Carbon monoxide has a residence time in the atmosphere of one to four months. The relatively constant concentration, and the residence time, suggest efficient methods for the removal of carbon monoxide. These methods are outlined below.

Just above the tropopause carbon monoxide is removed by:

$$\cdot OH + CO \longrightarrow CO_2 + \cdot H \qquad (2.16)$$

Hydroxyl free radicals, $\cdot OH$, come from the photolysis of water

$$H_2O \xrightarrow{hf} \cdot OH + \cdot H \qquad (2.17)$$

and from

$$O^* + H_2O \longrightarrow 2\cdot OH \qquad (2.18)$$

The energy-rich (excited state) oxygen atoms, O^*, are formed by the photolysis of ozone:

$$O_3 \xrightarrow{hf} O_2 + O^* \qquad (2.19)$$

All species in *reactions 2.16* to *2.19* are in the gaseous state.

Reaction 2.16 also occurs in the troposphere and removes up to 50% of the carbon monoxide emitted into the atmosphere. The most important agents for the removal of tropospheric carbon monoxide are bacteria and fungi in the soil. This occurs at the interface between the soil and the air:

$$CO(g) + \tfrac{1}{2}O_2(g) \longrightarrow CO_2(g)$$
$$\text{by } \textit{Bacillus oligocarbophilus} \qquad (2.20)$$

$$4CO(g) + 2H_2O(l) \longrightarrow CH_4(g) + 3CO_2(g)$$
$$\text{by } \textit{Methanosarcina backerii} \qquad (2.21)$$

The uptake of carbon monoxide by soil bacteria is rapid and these bacteria have the ability to cope with around three times the present annual output of carbon monoxide from artificial sources.

Other ways in which carbon monoxide is removed are:

$$CO(g) + O(g) + M \longrightarrow CO_2(g) + M \qquad (2.23)$$

and conversion by plant leaves:

$$CO(g) + \text{plant leaves} \xrightarrow{hf} \underset{\text{aminoacids}}{NH_2CH(R)COOH} \qquad (2.24)$$

$$CO(g) + \text{plant leaves} \xrightarrow{night} CO_2(g) \qquad (2.25)$$

(M is some inert third body surface on which the two species come together.)

The level of carbon monoxide in congested urban areas is a problem because of its toxicity to human beings. Carbon monoxide combines with haemoglobin in the blood to form carboxyhaemoglobin. The bonding in this molecule is strong and the carbon monoxide is not easily released, so the haemoglobin is tied up and is not able to perform its usual function of transporting oxygen around the body. The effects of carbon monoxide poisoning are a reddening of the lips (cherry lips), unconsciousness and death by asphyxiation, depending on the degree of exposure. In rare cases carbon monoxide poisoning leads to Parkinson's disease. Carbon monoxide is doubly dangerous because it is odourless and colourless, so we cannot detect it with our senses until it may be too late.

The average level of carbon monoxide in the

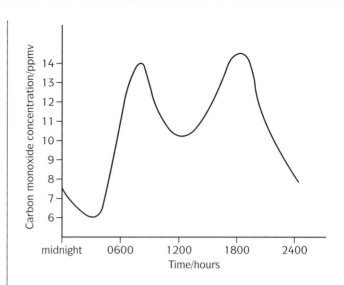

● *Figure 2.6* The 24-hour variation of carbon monoxide concentration in an urban area.

northern hemisphere is 0.13 ppmv and in the southern hemisphere it is 0.04 ppmv. In urban areas it is much higher. During the rush hour the concentration peaks twice at about 14 ppmv, as can be seen in *figure 2.6*. In congested traffic, carbon monoxide concentration can reach 300 ppmv (*figure 2.7*).

SAQ 2.5

Summarise the processes which remove carbon monoxide from the troposphere. Consider why these processes might not apply at urban street level.

● *Figure 2.7* Congested traffic in cities leads to a high level of carbon monoxide in the atmosphere.

Sulphur dioxide

Sulphur dioxide is a dangerous primary pollutant. It causes harm to people, plants and materials, and has been a major constituent of most air pollution disasters. The residence time of sulphur dioxide is 3–7 days, depending on the weather conditions: wet conditions will remove sulphur dioxide from the air more rapidly.

Each year about 150 million tonnes of sulphur dioxide are discharged into the atmosphere. Most of this comes from the burning of fossil fuels, particularly in the generation of electricity. Coal is the fuel mainly responsible, but some sulphur dioxide comes from the smelting of sulphide ores in the extraction of zinc, lead and copper. Sulphur in coal is converted to sulphur dioxide on combustion:

$$-S-(s) + O_2(g) \longrightarrow SO_2(g) \qquad (2.26)$$
in compound

There is less sulphur in crude oil, but it is concentrated in the heavy fuel oil fraction during refining. It is this fraction which is used in oil-fired power stations. The petrol which is used in cars and other vehicles contains about 0.05% sulphur.

The ambient concentration of sulphur dioxide in non-industrial areas is roughly 0.1 ppbv (parts per billion by volume). In cities maximum levels occur in winter due to an increase in the burning of fossil fuels.

Oxidation of sulphur dioxide

Sulphur dioxide in the atmosphere is oxidised to sulphur trioxide, a secondary pollutant, which then reacts with water to form sulphuric acid. The oxidation of sulphur dioxide in the atmosphere can occur in three ways: free-radical oxidation, catalysis and photochemical oxidation.

Catalysis

The overall oxidation reaction is summarised by the equation:

$$2SO_2(g) + 2H_2O(l) + O_2(g) \longrightarrow 2H_2SO_4(aq);$$
$$\Delta H = -600\,kJ \qquad (2.27)$$

This reaction is slow, but is catalysed by aerosols containing metal ions, for example manganese(II),

iron(III) and copper(II), and the oxides of chromium, aluminium, lead and calcium. The metal ion catalysts work because of their variable oxidation number. The surfaces of buildings can act as catalytic centres, and a high humidity increases reaction rate. The sulphur dioxide is oxidised in water droplets and proceeds best at a pH greater than 7, so as sulphuric acid is produced the reaction slows down.

Aerosols

Aerosols are very small particles of liquid suspended in a gaseous medium. Particles range in size from 10 nm to 10 μm. The particles are prevented from coming together by charges on their surface.

When sulphur dioxide dissolves in the water droplet the reactions are:

$$SO_2(g) + H_2O(l) \rightleftharpoons H_2SO_3(aq) \qquad (2.28)$$

$$H_2SO_3(aq) + H_2O(l) \rightleftharpoons H_3O^+(aq) + HSO_3^-(aq) \qquad (2.29)$$

$$HSO_3^-(aq) + H_2O(l) \rightleftharpoons H_3O^+(aq) + SO_3^{2-}(aq) \qquad (2.30)$$

$$2HSO_3^-(aq) \rightleftharpoons S_2O_5^{2-}(aq) + H_2O(l) \qquad (2.31)$$

Reactions 2.29 and *2.30* show that the solubility of sulphur dioxide in the water droplet is reduced by increased acidity: additional $H^+(aq)$ ions move these reactions to the left and hence move *reaction 2.28* to the left.

The presence of ammonia increases the rate of oxidation by reducing the acidity, resulting in the formation of ammonium sulphate, $(NH_4)_2SO_4$, and ammonium hydrogensulphate, NH_4HSO_4, in the aerosols.

It is actually the hydrogensulphite ion, $HSO_3^-(aq)$, in the water droplet which is oxidised, rather than the sulphur dioxide directly:

$$HSO_3^-(aq) + H_2O(l) \\ \longrightarrow HSO_4^-(aq) + 2H^+(aq) + 2e^- \qquad (2.32)$$

The hydrogen ions formed are removed by reaction with oxygen:

$$O_2(g) + 4H^+(aq) + 4e^- \longrightarrow 2H_2O(l) \qquad (2.33)$$

Photochemical oxidation

Sulphur dioxide absorbs radiation producing an excited state:

$$SO_2 \xrightarrow{hf} SO_2^*$$ (2.34)

This has a relatively long lifetime and reacts in a variety of ways to give sulphur trioxide (all species in the gaseous state):

$$SO_2^* + O_2 \longrightarrow SO_3 + O^*$$ (2.35)

$$SO_2^* + SO_2 \longrightarrow SO_3 + SO$$ (2.36)

$$SO + SO_2 \longrightarrow SO_3 + S$$ (2.37)

The oxidation of sulphur dioxide by this process is slow (0.1–0.2% per hour).

Other ways in which sulphur dioxide is oxidised are:

$$SO_2(g) + O_3(g) \longrightarrow SO_3(g) + O_2(g)$$ (2.38)

(this reaction is slow in the gas phase, but rapid in water droplets) and:

$$SO_2(g) + NO_2(g) \longrightarrow SO_3(g) + NO(g)$$ (2.39)

Thus you can see that nitrogen dioxide from motor vehicle emissions can increase the rate of oxidation of sulphur dioxide.

Acid rain

Acid rain is produced by sulphur dioxide dissolving in water to give sulphurous and sulphuric acids, H_2SO_3 and H_2SO_4. Pure rain-water has a pH of approximately 5.6, but sulphur dioxide emissions can cause it to fall as low as 2. Sulphur dioxide is the main cause of acid rain, but nitrogen oxide emissions from power stations and motor vehicles also contribute to its formation (the nitrogen oxides dissolve in water droplets by a series of complex reactions to form nitric acid).

Sulphur dioxide originating in the UK forms sulphuric acid aerosols, which are precipitated in Scandinavia; they increase the acidity of the lakes and destroy aquatic life. Acid rain also leaches nutrients from soils and enables many toxic metal ions to dissolve more readily in soil solution (see chapter 5). These ions may then enter the food chain: aluminium released into Scandinavian lakes causes the deaths of many fish. Acid rain increases the rate of corrosion of metals and buildings containing limestone or marble, and affects the growth of trees (*figure 2.8*).

Corrosion of buildings

Apart from its effects on the health of plants and animals, sulphur dioxide has a corrosive effect on many building materials, metals, paper and clothing fabrics.

The building materials limestone and marble are forms of calcium carbonate. These are attacked by both sulphur dioxide and sulphuric acid to form calcium sulphate $CaSO_4$:

$$CaCO_3(s) + SO_2(g) + \tfrac{1}{2}O_2(g) \longrightarrow CaSO_4(s) + CO_2(g)$$ (2.40)

$$CaCO_3(s) + H_2SO_4(aq) \longrightarrow CaSO_4(s) + H_2O(l) + CO_2(g)$$ (2.41)

As calcium sulphate is more soluble than calcium carbonate it will wash out and as a result the stone face will corrode.

● *Figure 2.8*

a Denuded spruce trees caused by acid rain in the Czech Republic.

b A statue damaged where the stone has been eroded by acid rain.

Another problem is that the calcium sulphate can dissolve in the moisture in cracks. The volume of one mole of calcium sulphate (the molar volume) is greater than the volume of one mole of calcium carbonate, so when moisture from the cracks evaporates, the calcium sulphate remaining occupies a greater volume than the calcium carbonate it has replaced. This causes expansion and stress in the stonework.

SAQ 2.6

a Given the following densities:

calcium carbonate (calcite), $CaCO_3$ $2.71 \, g \, cm^{-3}$

calcium sulphate (anhydrite), $CaSO_4$ $2.96 \, g \, cm^{-3}$

calcium sulphate (gypsum), $CaSO_4.2H_2O$ $2.32 \, g \, cm^{-3}$

calculate the molar volume of each substance.

b Using the figures you obtain, explain why stress forces are set up in the stonework when calcium sulphate replaces calcium carbonate.

Corrosion of metals

Sulphur dioxide greatly increases the rate of corrosion of metals. For example, iron:

$$Fe(s) + SO_2(g) + O_2(g) \longrightarrow FeSO_4(s) \qquad (2.42)$$

$$Fe(s) + H_2SO_4(aq) \longrightarrow FeSO_4(aq) + H_2(g) \qquad (2.43)$$

The formation of iron(II) sulphate enables ionic conduction to occur and speeds up the electro-chemical processes of corrosion. With other metals (for instance aluminium and copper), sulphuric acid dissolves their protective oxide layers, forming sulphates that are dissolved and washed away.

Effect on paper

The main constituent of paper is the natural polymer cellulose. Cellulose is a very long chain molecule composed of glucose units joined by a C–O–C link. Sulphur dioxide brings about acid hydrolysis of this link in the cellulose, causing the paper to become brittle.

Smog

Sulphur dioxide has been involved in most air pollution disasters where health has been seriously affected *(table 2.3)*. The mixture of smoke and fog which is associated with these disasters is termed **smog** *(figure 2.9)*.

Water, particulate material and sulphur dioxide are all necessary for the creation of smog; all these factors together produce a more serious effect than they do individually. They are said to act

● *Figure 2.9* The London smog of December 1952 caused more than 4000 deaths in five days.

Location	Date	Duration/days	Deaths
Meuse Valley, Liège, Belgium	December 1930	3	60
Donora, Pennsylvania, USA	October 1948	5	20
London, UK	December 1952	5	4000
	January 1956	3	1000
	December 1957	3	800
	December 1962	5	700
New York, USA	January to February 1963	15	400
	November 1966	3	168

● *Table 2.3* Major air pollution disasters

synergistically. The water vapour condenses on the particles, which also act as a large surface area for the catalytic oxidation of sulphur dioxide to sulphur trioxide. Sulphuric acid is formed in the small water droplets and can have a serious effect on plants and animals *(table 2.4)*. If these droplets penetrate the respiratory system, severe distress and death can result. Sulphur dioxide adsorbed onto particles can also be inhaled into the respiratory tract. It is then converted to sulphuric acid in the lungs. In either case this leads to the aggravation of such respiratory diseases as asthma, emphysema and chronic bronchitis. It also causes reduced lung function and irritation to the eyes and the respiratory tract. Sulphur dioxide also stimulates contraction of the airways, making it difficult to breathe. Any of these conditions can lead to death in the old and the weak *(figure 2.10)*.

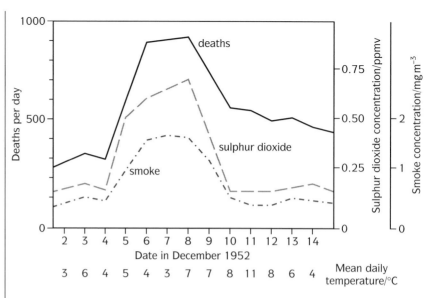

● *Figure 2.10* The correlation between deaths and air pollution in London, December 1952.

Sulphur dioxide destroys the leaf tissue in plants, because it inhibits the enzyme involved in photorespiration.

From studies conducted in large cities, the World Health Organization (WHO) recommends that concentrations of sulphur dioxide and smoke should remain below $100–150\,\mu g\,m^{-3}$ in any 24-hour period, and below a mean of $40–60\,\mu g\,m^{-3}$ in a year.

SAQ 2.7

Study *figure 2.10*. Draw conclusions about the correlation between smoke, sulphur dioxide levels, temperature and the number of deaths.

Subject	Effect	Concentration/ppmv	Exposure time
humans	odour	0.5–0.7	1 second
	taste	0.3–0.1	a few seconds
	epidemic occurrence of respiratory disease	0.2	24 hours
	affects heart and lungs	1.6	10 minutes
	discomfort	5.0	10 minutes
	severe distress	5.0–10.0	10 minutes
plants	bleached spots on edges of leaves and areas between leaf veins	0.28	24 hours
	yellowing of leaves, loss of chlorophyll (chlorosis)	0.25 (single concentration) or annual average of 0.3	
	growth suppressed	0.05–0.2	24 hours
animals	affects central nervous system	0.2	10 seconds on several occasions
	lethal	50.0	30 days at 6 hours a day

● *Table 2.4* Effect of sulphur dioxide on humans, plants and animals

Control of sulphur dioxide emission

The sulphur content of fuels can be reduced by various methods, all of which reduce the amount of sulphur dioxide released when fuels are burnt.

Coal contains two forms of sulphur. Inorganic sulphur present as metal sulphides (known as pyrites) can be removed from coal by crushing the coal to very small particles to expose the veins of pyrites, then mixing the ground coal with water in a large tank. Pyrites has a higher density than coal and therefore sinks faster. The cleaned coal is skimmed from the top of the tank.

Organic sulphur is bound to the carbon in coal. Treatment with 10% sodium hydroxide under pressure and at high temperature removes about half the organic sulphur, which remains in the liquid phase. The coal is then washed and dried.

Another process for removing organic sulphur is the solvent refining of coal. Ground coal is mixed with the solvent anthracene, in which 95% of the carbon dissolves. The solution is then treated with hydrogen at high temperature and pressure. The coal is recovered as a solid or as a liquid. The resulting coal has less than 1% ash and the sulphur content is reduced to below 1%. An added bonus is that the heating value per tonne of coal desulphured by this method is 30% greater than the original coal.

Sulphur in oil is removed by treatment with calcium oxide and then oxidation by heating in air:

$$3S(l) + 2CaO(s) \longrightarrow 2CaS(s) + SO_2(g) \quad (2.44)$$

$$2CaS(s) + 3O_2(g) \longrightarrow 2CaO(s) + 2SO_2(g) \quad (2.45)$$

The sulphur dioxide produced is used to make sulphuric acid by the contact process. In this process sulphur dioxide is mixed with oxygen from the air and passed over a catalyst at about 450°C. The sulphur dioxide is oxidised to sulphur trioxide, which is then dissolved to produce concentrated sulphuric acid. (Sulphuric acid has many uses throughout industry in the manufacture of fertilisers, detergents, dyestuffs, drugs, explosives and rayon (artificial silk).)

Sometimes sulphur in oil is removed by hydrogenation:

$$S(l) + H_2(g) \longrightarrow H_2S(g) \quad (2.46)$$

The hydrogen sulphide is removed in a process called scrubbing.

Gaseous sulphur dioxide emissions from power stations can be prevented by removing the sulphur dioxide from flue (chimney) gases. This *flue desulphurisation* is generally carried out using limestone-based fluidised beds. Coal is mixed with limestone and is layered on metal plates. The air for combustion comes from below, passing through holes in the metal plates. The air flow is so strong that the particles of coal and limestone are lifted and float above their bed on the plate. In this state the mixture behaves like a fluid, hence the name *fluidised bed*. The limestone reacts with sulphur dioxide from the burning coal to form fine particles of calcium sulphate:

$$CaCO_3(s) \overset{heat}{\longrightarrow} CaO(s) + CO_2(g) \quad (2.47)$$

$$CaO(s) + SO_2(g) + \tfrac{1}{2}O_2(g) \longrightarrow CaSO_4(s) \quad (2.48)$$

The sulphate particles are carried off in the flue gases and are removed by electrostatic precipitation.

Calcium sulphate can be used to make sulphuric acid. Other bases such as magnesium oxide and ammonia are sometimes used. Again the end product can be used to make sulphuric acid.

Another advantage of the fluidised bed technique is that the temperature of the burning coal is lower than that of coal burnt in a normal boiler. A consequence of this is that fewer nitrogen oxides are formed. Thus two forms of atmospheric pollution are reduced.

Hydrogen sulphide

Hydrogen sulphide, H_2S, is emitted from volcanoes and is also produced during the decay of organic material occurring in the absence of air. Bacterial reduction of sulphate ions also gives rise to hydrogen sulphide:

$$SO_4{}^{2-}(aq) + 2H^+(aq) + 2[CH_2O](aq)$$
$$\underset{\text{sugars}}{\longrightarrow} H_2S(g) + 2CO_2(g) + 2H_2O(l) \quad (2.49)$$

Nearly all the hydrogen sulphide in the atmosphere is produced in this way (98 million tonnes a year). Approximately one-third of the hydrogen sulphide produced naturally comes from the oceans and two-thirds from the land. Artificial sources are paper manufacture, rayon production and oil refining.

Hydrogen sulphide is very toxic, but is oxidised rapidly in the air by small traces of ozone:

$$H_2S(g) + O_3(g) \longrightarrow H_2O(g) + SO_2(g) \qquad (2.50)$$

Oxides of nitrogen

The nitrogen oxides are serious pollutants in that, together with hydrocarbons, they are responsible for photochemical air pollution such as that which occurs in the city of Los Angeles. They also contribute to the formation of acid rain. The main artificial sources of nitrogen oxide emissions are shown in *figure 2.11*.

Nitrogen can have a variety of oxidation numbers in its oxides:

NO_3^-, HNO_3	$+5$
$2NO_2 \rightleftharpoons N_2O_4$	$+4$
NO_2^-, HNO_2	$+3$
NO	$+2$
N_2O	$+1$

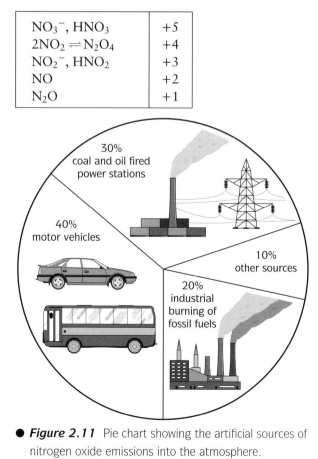

30%
coal and oil fired
power stations

40%
motor vehicles

10%
other sources

20%
industrial
burning of
fossil fuels

● *Figure 2.11* Pie chart showing the artificial sources of nitrogen oxide emissions into the atmosphere.

The main pollutant oxides nitrogen monoxide, NO, and nitrogen dioxide, NO_2, are frequently considered together, and are referred to as NO_x.

Nitrogen itself, N_2, has an oxidation number of 0. It is stable and has low reactivity. However, at high temperature it will combine with oxygen to form nitrogen monoxide:

$$N_2(g) + O_2(g) \rightleftharpoons 2NO(g);$$
$$\Delta H = +180 \, kJ \, mol^{-1} \qquad (2.51)$$

At 298 K, the position of equilibrium is well to the left, but at the high temperatures in an internal combustion engine (say 2000 K) significantly more nitrogen monoxide is produced. Exhaust gases cool rapidly and this prevents the nitrogen monoxide from decomposing, so nitrogen monoxide is a primary pollutant.

Nitrogen dioxide is formed by reaction of nitrogen monoxide with oxygen. It is therefore a secondary pollutant.

$$2NO(g) + O_2(g) \longrightarrow 2NO_2(g) \qquad (2.52)$$

Two molecules of nitrogen dioxide join together or *dimerise*, particularly at lower temperatures:

$$2NO_2(g) \rightleftharpoons \underset{\text{dimer}}{N_2O_4(g)}$$

It is estimated that annual emissions of nitrogen oxides are 53 million tonnes from artificial sources and 1092 million tonnes from natural sources (*Air Pollution Control Association Journal*, **20**, 303). You can see that far more comes from natural processes, for example biological activity in soil, volcanoes and lightning, than comes from the activities of people. The problem with artificial emissions is that they are concentrated in urban areas and can reach high concentrations. The biggest source is the combustion of coal (51%), followed by oil and petrol combustion.

Power stations and transport are the biggest contributors by far to artificial nitrogen oxide pollution. Urban levels follow seasonal variations: the concentration of NO_x is significantly higher in winter. Over a 24-hour period, high concentrations of NO_x coincide with the morning and evening traffic peaks.

Photochemical smog

Photochemical smog is a whitish yellow haze containing chemical species which irritate the respiratory tract, causing long-term effects on health *(table 2.5)*.

The chemical pollutants in photochemical smog are nitrogen monoxide, nitrogen dioxide, hydrocarbons, peroxyethanoyl nitrate (PAN), ozone and aldehydes. Nitrogen monoxide and hydrocarbons are the primary pollutants.

The conditions needed for photochemical smog to form are a particular combination of atmospheric pollutants, sunlight, a stable temperature inversion, and land enclosed by hills. Such conditions occur in Los Angeles in the summer months. In that city 68% of nitrogen oxide emissions arise from vehicle exhausts.

Figure 2.12 shows that the concentrations of the primary pollutants rise during the early-morning rush hour. Nitrogen dioxide builds up as nitrogen monoxide is oxidised. Later, the concentration of nitrogen dioxide falls due to photolysis in a complex series of reactions, which leads to the

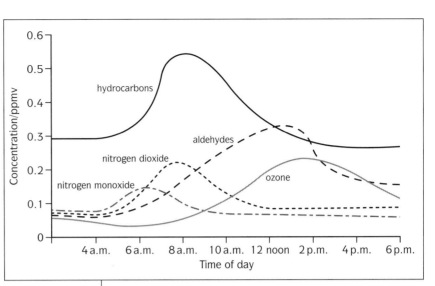

● *Figure 2.12* The variation in concentration of atmospheric pollutants during daylight hours in Los Angeles.

formation of ozone, aldehydes and peroxynitrates. Nitrous and nitric acids, HNO_2 and HNO_3, are formed by the reaction of nitrogen oxides with water, and are removed by rain or by aerosol formation. Nitrogen oxides and hydrocarbons produced in the afternoon rush hour are removed by reaction with ozone, leading to a drop in ozone concentration. Ozone in the lower atmosphere is an extremely dangerous pollutant (see page 23).

Subject	Pollutant	Effect	Concentration/ ppmv	Exposure time/ hours
humans	nitrogen dioxide	odour	1.0–3.0	
		lethal	500.0	48
	ozone	odour	0.005–0.05	
		irritation of throat	0.1	2
		shortness of breath	0.4–1.0	2
		irritation of eyes and nose	0.1	1
		impaired lung function, chest pains, coughing	1.5–2.0	2
		unconsciousness	11.0	0.25
		death	50.0	1
	PAN	reduced lung function	0.3	0.20
	HCHO	odour	0.1	
		severe distress	10.0–20.0	
plants	nitrogen dioxide	leaf lesions	2.5	4
		inhibits photosynthesis	0.6	
	ozone	leaf lesions, inhibits photosynthesis	0.1	2–4
	PAN	collapse of young cells	0.01	6
	HCHO	leaf symptoms	0.2	48

● *Table 2.5* Effects of pollutants in photochemical smog

The formation of photochemical smog proceeds by several steps. You will see that there are many free radicals (see page 6). (Atmospheric free radicals are species rarely encountered in laboratory chemistry.) The principle reactions are as follows.

■ **Production of nitrogen monoxide**

This occurs at high temperature in an internal combustion engine. (M is another molecule that helps the reaction to take place.)

$$O_2 + M \rightleftharpoons O + O + M \qquad (2.54)$$

$$N_2 + M \rightleftharpoons N\cdot + N\cdot + M \qquad (2.55)$$

The combination of *reactions 2.54* and *2.55* is written as:

$$N_2 + O_2 \rightleftharpoons 2NO\cdot \qquad (2.56)$$

Further reactions are:

$$RH + O \longrightarrow R\cdot + \cdot OH \qquad (2.57)$$

$$N\cdot + \cdot OH \longrightarrow NO\cdot + H\cdot \qquad (2.58)$$

$$CO + \cdot OH \longrightarrow CO_2 + H\cdot \qquad (2.59)$$

$$H\cdot + O_2 \longrightarrow \cdot OH + O \qquad (2.60)$$

All species mentioned in the above sequence are in the gaseous state. RH represents a hydrocarbon, R· a hydrocarbon free radical. You can see that hydroxyl radicals, ·OH, play an important part in the formation of nitrogen monoxide.

■ **Production of nitrogen dioxide**

All species discussed are in the gaseous state.

The direct oxidation of nitrogen monoxide to nitrogen dioxide

$$2NO\cdot + O_2 \rightleftharpoons 2NO_2\cdot \qquad (2.61)$$

is slow at atmospheric concentrations. An important reaction for the oxidation of nitrogen monoxide is:

$$NO\cdot + HO_2\cdot \longrightarrow NO_2\cdot + \cdot OH \qquad (2.62)$$

$HO_2\cdot$ is a free radical present in the atmosphere. The rapid conversion of nitrogen monoxide to nitrogen dioxide is explained by photochemical reactions involving ozone. Nitrogen dioxide is able to absorb radiation in the visible and ultraviolet regions. This radiation breaks the N–O bond, which has an energy of $300\,kJ\,mol^{-1}$:

$$NO_2\cdot \overset{hf}{\longrightarrow} NO\cdot + O \qquad (2.63)$$

The oxygen atoms produced then react with diatomic oxygen in the presence of some third body, M, to form ozone:

$$O + O_2 + M \longrightarrow O_3 + M \qquad (2.64)$$

M can be any gas molecule that is able to carry off the excess energy. In the atmosphere this is mainly molecular nitrogen and oxygen.

This ozone can then oxidise nitrogen monoxide to nitrogen dioxide:

$$NO\cdot + O_3 \longrightarrow NO_2\cdot + O_2 \qquad (2.65)$$

Reactions 2.64 and *2.65* are both fast.

These reactions show that nitrogen dioxide is involved in both the formation and the destruction of ozone. The net result of this is an ozone level in the troposphere in equilibrium with the levels of nitrogen monoxide and nitrogen dioxide, and dependent upon the levels of solar radiation.

■ **Production of hydrocarbon radicals**

Hydrocarbons, RCH_3, in the atmosphere react with hydroxyl radicals to produce hydrocarbon radicals, $RCH_2\cdot$:

$$RCH_3 + \cdot OH \longrightarrow RCH_2\cdot + H_2O \qquad (2.66)$$

Among the hydrocarbons it is the alkenes which are the most reactive. In Los Angeles, it is estimated that 1730 tonnes of hydrocarbons are input into the atmosphere every day, and 16% are alkenes.

The free radicals produced in *reaction 2.66* are very reactive and immediately become involved in other reactions. For example:

$$RCH_2\cdot + O_2 \longrightarrow RCH_2O_2\cdot \qquad (2.67)$$
$$\text{peroxyl radical}$$

This peroxyl radical can oxidise nitrogen monoxide to nitrogen dioxide:

$$RCH_2O_2\cdot + NO\cdot \longrightarrow RCH_2O\cdot + NO_2\cdot \qquad (2.68)$$

This alternative reaction for the oxidation of nitrogen monoxide reduces the need for ozone.

The nitrogen dioxide produced in *reaction 2.68* can react photochemically by *reactions 2.63* and *2.64* to produce more ozone. Hence the presence of hydrocarbons leads to the production of ozone. This has been shown to occur in smog chamber studies, in which attempts are made to simulate atmospheric conditions in closed laboratory chambers.

■ **Production of aldehydes**
Aldehydes are formed by the reaction of $RCH_2O\cdot$ radicals with an oxygen molecule:

$$RCH_2O\cdot + O_2 \longrightarrow RCHO + HO_2\cdot \qquad (2.69)$$

You will remember that the hydroperoxyl radical $HO_2\cdot$ was also important in the oxidation of nitrogen monoxide *(reaction 2.62)*.

■ **Production of peroxy compounds**
Peroxy compounds such as peroxyethanoyl nitrate (old name peroxyacetyl nitrate or PAN) have serious effects on health, irritating the respiratory system and the eyes.

$$\underset{\underset{\text{(from aldehydes)}}{O}}{RC\overset{\parallel}{O}O\cdot} + NO_2\cdot \longrightarrow \underset{\underset{\text{peroxyethanoyl nitrate}}{O}}{RC\overset{\parallel}{O}OONO_2} \qquad (2.70)$$

The threshold for eye irritation is only 700 ppbv (parts per billion by volume) for PAN and 5 ppbv for peroxybenzoyl nitrate, PBzN. Substances which irritate the eye in this way are said to be *lachrymatory*.
Reaction of ozone with alkenes in the atmosphere produces an aldehyde or ketone and a peroxyl radical:

$$RCH{=}CH_2 + O_3 \longrightarrow RCHO\cdot + H_2COO\cdot \qquad (2.71)$$
$$\text{or} \quad RCHOO\cdot + \underset{\text{methanal}}{H_2CO\cdot}$$

The peroxyl radical formed is available for further oxidation of the nitrogen monoxide, as in *reaction 2.68*, and for the formation of PAN, *reaction 2.70*.

Therefore we have a complex series of reactions in which the oxides of nitrogen play a key part.

SAQ 2.8
Design a chart showing how the reactions in photochemical smog are interlinked.

Ozone

We saw in chapter 1 that ozone in the stratosphere is essential in screening the Earth from dangerous ultraviolet radiation. Paradoxically, ozone present in the troposphere is a dangerous pollutant. Depending on concentration it can have a serious effect on health and vegetation.

Ozone plays a part in the complex series of reactions involved in photochemical smog (page 21). Its effects on health are listed in *table 2.5*. Increased ozone concentration in the troposphere arises from photochemical reactions of primary pollutants originating from motor vehicle emissions and incomplete combustion of fossil fuels.

The natural background level of ozone near the ground is 20–50 ppbv. This ozone is present mainly as a result of transport of air from the stratosphere due to atmospheric mixing processes. Ozone levels above background are produced by reactions with nitrogen oxides (see also page 6):

$$2NO\cdot + O_2 \longrightarrow 2NO_2\cdot \qquad (2.72)$$

$$NO_2\cdot \overset{hf}{\longrightarrow} NO\cdot + O \qquad (2.73)$$

$$O + O_2 + M \longrightarrow O_3 + M \qquad (2.74)$$

$$NO\cdot + O_3 \longrightarrow NO_2\cdot + O_2 \qquad (2.75)$$

M is any gas molecule that is able to carry off the excess energy of the reaction. All species are in the gaseous state. You can see that nitrogen oxides participate in both the formation and destruction of ozone.

The level of ozone in urban areas varies during a 24-hour period *(figure 2.12)*. You can see that the nitrogen monoxide produced from vehicle exhausts in the morning rush hour leads to a rise in the level of ozone via the formation of nitrogen dioxide.

SAQ 2.9
Explain in detail the variations shown in *figure 2.12* relating them to *reactions 2.72–2.75* and to light levels.

Seasonal variations in tropospheric ozone in the northern hemisphere are shown in *figure 2.13*. High levels in June, July and August relate to longer hours of daylight and greater intensity of sunshine. Apart from the effects on health and vegetation mentioned in *table 2.5*, ozone in the troposphere has other detrimental effects.

■ Ozone will add across unsaturated carbon bonds to produce breakdown products. Common synthetic materials containing unsaturated carbon bonds are found in plastics, paints and dyes. Rubber is a polymer containing a carbon–carbon double bond:

$$-\left[CH_2-\underset{\underset{CH_3}{|}}{C}=CH-CH_2\right]_n-$$

It is made from the monomer:

$$H_2C=\underset{\underset{CH_3}{|}}{C}-CH=CH_2$$

Ozone adds across the C=C bond to form an ozonide which breaks down to give carbonyl groups:

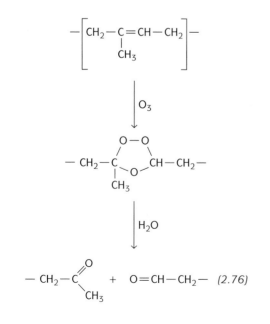

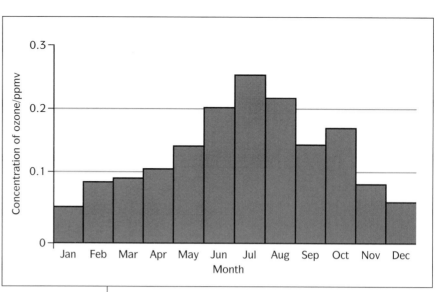

● **Figure 2.13** The seasonal variation in tropospheric ozone in the Northern Hemisphere.

Reaction 2.76 causes rubber to crack, creating damage to car tyres.

■ Ozone absorbs infrared radiation emitted at the Earth's surface, so tropospheric ozone contributes to the 'greenhouse effect'. If the present tropospheric ozone level were to double, the average surface temperature of the Earth would increase by about 1 °C.

SAQ 2.10

Give the systematic name of the rubber monomer.

Measuring ozone levels

Ozone levels in the troposphere down to 10 ppbv can be detected by the oxidation of potassium iodide followed by measurement of the concentration of iodine formed. Levels down to 1 ppbv can be detected by the light produced in the reaction of ozone with ethene.

In the USA, the level at which tropospheric ozone is likely to cause damage to health has been defined as an exposure to a concentration of 120 ppbv for 1 hour. Levels in excess of this figure have been recorded in Britain during the summer months in urban, suburban and rural sites.

SAQ 2.11

Ozone is a secondary pollutant. Explain what this means. Refer back to the reactions which lead to the formation of ozone in the troposphere and suggest methods for ozone control, giving chemical detail to your answer.

Ammonia

Ammonia is emitted naturally in biological decay and from animal excrement. The largest source of ammonia is thought to be animal urine. These natural emissions exceed 100 Tg (100 million tonnes) per year. Artificial emissions are relatively small and originate mainly from waste treatment. The residence time of ammonia is approximately 2 days.

Aerosols (see page 15) of ammonium salts form in acidic conditions and these are important in smog formation. For example:

$$2NH_3(g) + H_2SO_4(aq) \longrightarrow (NH_4)_2SO_4(aq) \quad (2.77)$$

Hence one product of the oxidation of sulphur dioxide in the atmosphere is the aerosol ammonium sulphate.

Ozone in the air oxidises ammonia to dinitrogen oxide, N_2O, nitrogen, N_2, and ammonium nitrate, NH_4NO_3. In hot weather there is significant dissociation of ammonium nitrate into ammonia and nitric acid.

The internal combustion engine

The motor vehicle has brought many benefits. Think of life without it! Unfortunately there is a price to pay in terms of atmospheric pollution.

Pollutants emitted from the internal combustion engine are particulates, carbon monoxide, oxides of nitrogen, oxides of sulphur, hydrocarbons and lead *(table 2.6)*. Most of these pollutants are emitted from the exhaust. From November 1991 these emissions have been checked in the annual

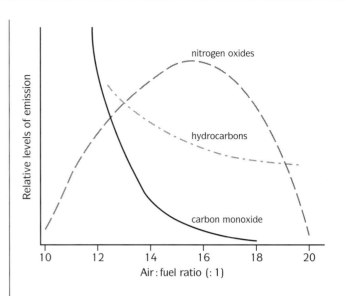

● *Figure 2.14* Exhaust emissions at various air : fuel ratios.

MoT test in the UK. The limits on emissions were set in an EU directive, and require motor vehicles to produce less than 2.72 g of carbon monoxide and 0.97 g of hydrocarbons and nitrogen oxides when they are tested. However, a significant amount of hydrocarbon pollution comes from the crankcase, carburettor and fuel tank.

The engine draws a mixture of fuel and air into the combustion chamber, where it is ignited. The hot gases present after ignition are then expelled before a new charge is introduced. In the petrol engine ignition is initiated by a sparking plug. In the diesel engine the mixture ignites spontaneously on compression. The air : fuel ratio plays an important part in determining the relative emissions of pollutants *(figure 2.14)*. The most common ratios used are between 12 : 1 and 15 : 1.

The stoichiometric ratio is 15 : 1. (*Stoichiometric* means the same ratio as in the chemical equation.) At this ratio you can see that emissions of nitrogen oxides are high, and those of carbon monoxide

Fuel	Carbon monoxide	Volatile organic compounds	Nitrogen oxides	Sulphur dioxide	Black smoke
petrol	236	25	29	0.9	0.6
DERV	10	17	59	3.8	18.0

● *Table 2.6* Emission factors for motor vehicles, measured in grams of pollutant produced per kilogram of fuel

and hydrocarbons are low. To reduce nitrogen oxide emissions, and to keep emissions of carbon monoxide and hydrocarbons low, a high air:fuel ratio should be used. When there is more air than the stoichiometric ratio it is referred to as a 'lean' mixture. The trouble is that a lean mixture will lead to misfiring. A richer mix (a lower air:fuel ratio) than 15:1 reduces nitrogen oxides but increases carbon monoxide and hydrocarbons.

Let us study the relationship between air:fuel ratio and power obtained (*figure 2.15*). A balance has to be made between power produced, fuel consumed and pollutants emitted. You can see that the maximum power is obtained at an air:fuel ratio of about 12.5:1. *Figure 2.14* shows that this produces high carbon monoxide and hydrocarbon emissions and low nitrogen oxide emissions. For low fuel consumption (16:1), high amounts of nitrogen oxides and low amounts of carbon monoxide and hydrocarbons are emitted.

Modern engine technology has produced 'lean-burn' engines which use an air:fuel ratio of 18:1. These engines have specially designed combustion chambers and electronically controlled fuel injection to overcome the problem of misfiring.

Emissions also depend on engine speed as shown in *table 2.7*. Acceleration produces the most nitrogen oxides, whereas deceleration leads to high hydrocarbon and carbon monoxide levels in the exhaust gases.

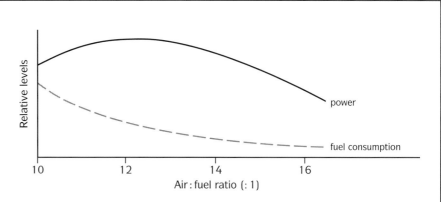

● *Figure 2.15* The relationship between air:fuel ratio, power production and fuel consumption.

Engine speed	Hydrocarbons/ppmv	NO$_x$/ppmv	CO/%
cruise	200–800	1000–3000	1–7
idle	500–1000	10–15	4–9
accelerate	50–800	1000–4000	0–8
decelerate	3000–12 000	5–50	2–9

● *Table 2.7* Exhaust emissions and engine speed

● *Figure 2.16* A typical catalytic converter, cut away to show the open honeycomb structure of the monolithic ceramic support coated with platinum-group metals.

Catalytic converters

Exhaust emissions can be controlled by the use of catalytic converters fitted to exhaust systems (*figure 2.16*). Hot exhaust gases are mixed with air and passed over a mixture of platinum, rhodium and palladium on a supporting honeycomb structure, which gives a very large surface area for the exhaust gases to come into contact with the catalyst. There are two forms of catalyst system:

■ an oxidation catalyst, which can be used in conjunction with 'lean-burn' engines to control carbon monoxide and hydrocarbon emissions. Hydrocarbons and carbon monoxide are rapidly oxidised to carbon dioxide and water at lower temperatures than normal (200–250 °C);

■ three-way catalysts, which will work with conventional engines to control carbon monoxide, hydrocarbon and nitrogen oxide emissions. The nitrogen oxides are reduced to nitrogen.

Catalytic converters enable an air:fuel ratio of 15:1, which gives maximum economy, the pollutants being rapidly removed by the converter. If the mixture is richer than this there is not enough oxygen in the exhaust for the carbon monoxide and hydrocarbons to be completely oxidised. Cars fitted with three-way systems have oxygen sensors in their exhaust gases that feed back to the electronically controlled fuel injection units, so that the air:fuel ratio can be optimised.

The presence of rhodium in the catalyst enables it to start working at 150 °C. Most engines attain an exhaust gas temperature of 200 °C within 30 seconds from a cold start, so the rhodium is an important factor in reducing emissions.

Catalytic converters have been installed in the majority of cars in the USA since the late 1970s. In the EU all cars manufactured after January 1993 have had to be fitted with catalytic converters by law. Catalytic converters are damaged by lead and hence can be used only in cars running on unleaded petrol.

CFCs

CFCs (chlorofluorocarbons or freons) were used extensively in aerosol cans, refrigerators and plastics until the late 1980s. There has been much concern about the effect of CFCs on the ozone in the stratosphere and this has led to a reduction in their use as aerosol propellants. They were used because of their lack of reactivity, low flammability and low toxicity. These properties made them ideal for the uses described.

CFCs are unaffected by ultraviolet radiation in the troposphere, but they are susceptible to attack in the stratosphere and release chlorine atoms.

Chlorine atoms in the stratosphere react with methane to form hydrogen chloride, HCl, or with ozone to produce chlorine monoxide, ClO. This chlorine monoxide then reacts with nitrogen monoxide radicals to form chlorine nitrate. This is a natural cycle which has been occurring for hundreds of millions of years. The chlorine atoms in nature come from chloromethane, CH_3Cl, which is given off from seaweed, the oceans and burning wood. During this time a balance of ozone in the stratosphere has been maintained.

The problem now is the quantity of CFCs reaching the stratosphere and the length of time they remain there due to their unreactivity. This leads to more ozone being destroyed than is created, as can be seen in the following reactions. (All species are in the gaseous state.)

■ **Initiation of ozone-destroying species** (wavelength of radiation required = 175–220 nm):

$$CCl_2F_2 \xrightarrow{hf} \cdot CClF_2 + Cl\cdot \quad (2.78)$$

$$CCl_3F \xrightarrow{hf} \cdot CCl_2F + Cl\cdot \quad (2.79)$$

■ **Propagation:**

$$Cl\cdot + O_3 \longrightarrow ClO\cdot + O_2 \quad (2.80)$$

$Cl\cdot$ is regenerated by reaction with oxygen atoms and nitrogen monoxide:

$$ClO\cdot + O \longrightarrow Cl\cdot + O_2 \quad (2.81)$$

$$ClO\cdot + NO\cdot \longrightarrow Cl\cdot + NO_2\cdot \quad (2.82)$$

This $Cl\cdot$ can then react with more ozone (*reaction 2.80*), this time leading to a loss of ozone without the absorption of radiation.

■ **Termination of cycle** (M is some inert third body):

$$Cl\cdot + CH_4 \longrightarrow HCl + \cdot CH_3 \quad (2.83)$$

$$Cl\cdot + H_2 \longrightarrow HCl + H\cdot \quad (2.84)$$

$$ClO\cdot + NO_2\cdot + M \longrightarrow ClNO_3 + M \quad (2.85)$$
$$\text{chlorine nitrate}$$

Reactions 2.83–2.85 remove the ozone-destroying species $Cl\cdot$ and $ClO\cdot$ from the atmosphere, so they are atmospheric sinks. The hydrogen chloride formed diffuses down to the troposphere, where it dissolves in water and is washed out in rain.

Chlorine nitrate cannot react with ozone, but it does undergo photolysis:

$$ClNO_3 \xrightarrow{hf} Cl\cdot + NO_3\cdot \qquad (2.86)$$

$$Cl\cdot + NO_3\cdot \longrightarrow ClO\cdot + NO_2\cdot \qquad (2.87)$$

$$ClO\cdot + NO_2\cdot \longrightarrow ClNO_2 + O \qquad (2.88)$$

Thus chlorine nitrate is only a temporary sink for chlorine atoms.

There is concern that these reactions will lead to a thinning of the ozone layer and hence an increased level of ultraviolet radiation reaching the Earth's surface. The consequences of ozone depletion in the stratosphere will be a cooling of the stratosphere and an increase in the temperature of the troposphere. Ironically this decrease of ozone levels in the stratosphere will lead to an increase in ozone levels in the troposphere.

To predict the precise consequences requires three-dimensional atmospheric modelling on an enormous scale. Very powerful computers using programs of immense complexity are used to simulate possible atmospheric changes as a result of pollution. Monitoring the problem is made more difficult by the natural changes in the ozone layer. The thickness of the layer varies with time and in space. Holes come and go. Levels are lower in winter and at night due to lack of sunshine. The British Antarctic Survey reported a hole in the ozone layer in 1985. More recently levels of ozone depletion in the Arctic have been found to be fifty times greater than scientists predicted.

The hole in the Antarctic is caused by unusual conditions. Most ozone is created at the tropics and transported to the poles. Climatic conditions in spring effectively cut off a cone of air over the South Pole from the surrounding atmosphere. Air in this cone becomes very cold and clouds of acidic ice crystals form in the stratosphere. Chlorine gas is released from chlorine nitrate:

$$HCl + ClNO_3(g) \longrightarrow HNO_3 + Cl_2(g) \qquad (2.89)$$
$$\text{in ice crystals} \qquad\qquad\qquad \text{in ice crystals}$$

When the Sun reappears in the polar spring, the air warms up and different chemical reactions occur, the most important of these being:

$$Cl_2 \xrightarrow{hf} Cl\cdot + Cl\cdot \qquad (2.90)$$

$$ClNO_3 \xrightarrow{hf} Cl\cdot + \cdot NO_3 \qquad (2.91)$$

$$H\cdot + \cdot NO_3 \longrightarrow HNO_3 \qquad (2.92)$$
$$\text{absorbed by clouds}$$

$Cl\cdot$ reacts with ozone as mentioned previously.

The Antarctic hole was mapped using both the Total Ozone Mapping Spectraphotometer (TOMS) on the Nimbus 7 Satellite and overflights by aircraft *(figure 2.17)*.

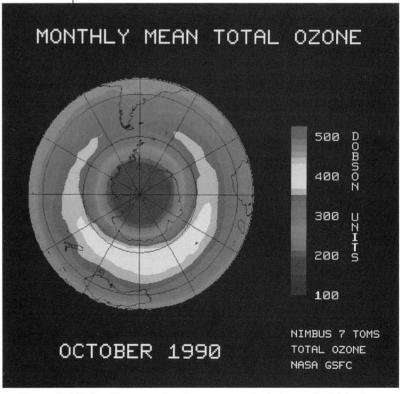

● *Figure 2.17* Satellite map showing a severe depletion or 'hole' in the ozone layer over Antarctica in October 1990. The hole is probably due to the pollution of the atmosphere by chlorofluorocarbons (CFCs) used in aerosols and refrigerants. First seen in 1979, the hole has grown each year since. It reaches a maximum in October, the Antarctic spring.

There are now controls on CFCs in the form of the Montreal Protocol, agreed in 1987 and tightened further in 1990. Fifty nations have agreed to restrict production and consumption of CFCs to 1986 levels, decreasing to 50% of 1986 levels by July 1998. However, because CFCs remain unreacted for 50–80 years, atmospheric modellers predict that it will take up to 100 years for existing CFCs to disperse. Meanwhile a search for substitutes is being made. The most likely candidates are the hydrofluorocarbons, HFCs, and hydrochlorofluorocarbons, HCFCs. These molecules contain C–H bonds that are broken down in the troposphere. Unfortunately both these types of compound are 'greenhouse gases' and may contribute to global warming.

Effects of ozone depletion

Thinning of the ozone layer results in more ultraviolet radiation of wavelengths below 320 nm reaching the Earth's surface. Ultraviolet radiation in the wavelength range 290–320 nm is known as ultraviolet-B. In living tissue this is absorbed by nucleic acids and may affect genetic information, leading to increased skin cancers in humans. Fair-skinned people are much more likely to develop skin cancers since they do not have the pigments that are present in dark skin which help to screen out the ultraviolet rays. Some predictions suggest that a 1% decrease in stratospheric ozone causes a 2% increase in ultraviolet-B and a 2–5% increase in skin cancer. Another effect of ultraviolet-B is that it appears to prevent normal immune responses in the skin and other parts of the body. Large ozone depletions, and hence increased ultraviolet radiation, will also affect crop yields in plants due to cell damage.

Larvae of fish, shrimp and crab, zooplankton (tiny animals) and phytoplankton (microscopic plants) are particularly affected by ultraviolet. Indeed a significant increase in the levels of ultraviolet radiation reaching the oceans could cause some microscopic life-forms to become extinct. Plankton are very important as they are the beginning of the food chain for all animals living in the sea. Phytoplankton give out oxygen into the water and into the atmosphere. Phytoplankton need only water, dissolved carbon dioxide, salts and sunlight to make all their vital substances. Zooplankton feed on these microscopic plants and are in turn eaten by fish. The fish are then eaten by humans and other animals. The effects of an upset in the ecological balance of plankton would be passed up the food chain and would be profound.

SAQ 2.12

Give the property of CFCs which led to their widespread use and has led to their long-term presence in the stratosphere.

SAQ 2.13

Summarise in five equations the ways in which CFCs lead to the loss of ozone in the stratosphere.

Radioactive pollution

There is increasing awareness of the dangers of exposure to naturally occurring radon gas, which is radioactive. Radon-222, ^{222}Rn, is colourless and odourless and results from the decay of uranium-238, ^{238}U. Radon-222 decays to a series of alpha-emitting daughters. (The products of decay of a particular radioactive isotope are known as the **daughter products**.) The inhalation of radon and its daughters is responsible for a major proportion of the overall annual dose of ionising radiation received by inhabitants of the United Kingdom. The highest levels of radon are found in Devon and Cornwall. Here the bedrock is granite that contains high concentrations of uranium.

In 1990 the National Radiological Protection Board (NRPB) set an advisory limit for radon concentration in homes of 200 becquerel per cubic metre. A 1988 survey by the NRPB revealed that about 50 000 houses in the UK exceeded this limit. Radon concentration in homes can be controlled by sealing floors, increasing ventilation and removing decay products by electrostatic precipitation.

Nuclear accidents have also released radioactive pollution into the air. In 1986 an explosion at the Chernobyl nuclear power station in the Ukraine (at that time part of the Soviet Union) released many dangerous radio-isotopes into the air. The most dangerous radio-isotopes are strontium-90, which accumulates in the bones and has a half-life of 27 years, iodine-129 and iodine-131, which concentrate in the thyroid gland, and caesium-137, which is taken up by muscle tissue. These isotopes are absorbed by grasses which are then eaten by animals. As a precaution after the Chernobyl accident, farmers in affected areas, including parts of Britain, were forbidden to send sheep and cows to market or to sell their milk.

SUMMARY

■ Pollution of the atmosphere is caused mainly by industrial and motor-vehicle emissions.

■ Primary pollutants are the original gases or particulates emitted.

■ Secondary pollutants are formed by reactions involving primary pollutants.

■ The main primary pollutants are carbon dioxide, carbon monoxide, sulphur dioxide and nitrogen oxides.

■ Secondary pollutants, formed mainly by photochemical processes, are ozone, peroxyethanoyl nitrate or PAN and methanal.

■ The use of catalytic converters in vehicle exhaust systems will enable maximum fuel economy and oxidation of carbon monoxide and hydrocarbon emissions.

■ CFCs were used in fridges and aerosols because of their inactivity. This same inactivity enables them to reach the stratosphere, where they cause destruction of ozone.

■ There is a hazard caused by radioactive pollution of the air, due to both radon emission from uranium-bearing rocks and nuclear accidents.

Questions

1 Discussion on the causes of global warming centres around additional emissions into the atmosphere caused by human activity.
   a Describe **two** important ways in which gases containing carbon are emitted into the atmosphere.
   b Name **two** emissions which contribute to global warming but which do not contain carbon.
   c Explain briefly how increased concentrations of carbon dioxide may contribute to global warming.
   d Give balanced equations for **two** chemical reactions by which carbon dioxide is removed from the atmosphere.

2 Los Angeles has, on average, a temperature inversion every other day.
   a What is meant by temperature inversion in this context?
   b What **two** harmful consequences follow from these temperature inversions and why?
   c Explain why these consequences are most apparent in the middle of the day, and not at peak traffic periods.

Chapter three

The hydrosphere

By the end of this chapter you should be able to:

1 describe and explain the water cycle and its place in the natural chemistry of the Earth;

2 describe the sources of dissolved elements in natural water;

3 explain the processes leading to the alkalinity of natural water;

4 discuss the principles of physical chemistry which apply at the interface between air and water.

● *Figure 3.1* Water is essential to life on Earth.

The waters of the Earth are essential to its functioning at all levels. From climate and geology to the minute cells of life, the presence of water plays a fundamental role in our environment. Water affects the world's weather patterns, it stores heat and transfers power, it forms the basis of the natural chemistry of the Earth, and life itself is dependent on the ready availability of water of good quality *(figure 3.1)*.

The water cycle

On the Earth's surface there are 1500 million cubic kilometres of water. Of this 98.3% is in the oceans and 1.6% is frozen as ice. The remainder is ground water with a small quantity in lakes and rivers. This water goes through a series of changes known as the **water cycle** *(figure 3.2)*.

Water passes into the atmosphere by evaporation from water surfaces and from plants (transpiration). When the water vapour reaches the cooler parts of the atmosphere it condenses to form clouds. The water then returns to the Earth's surface as rain or snow. About half of the

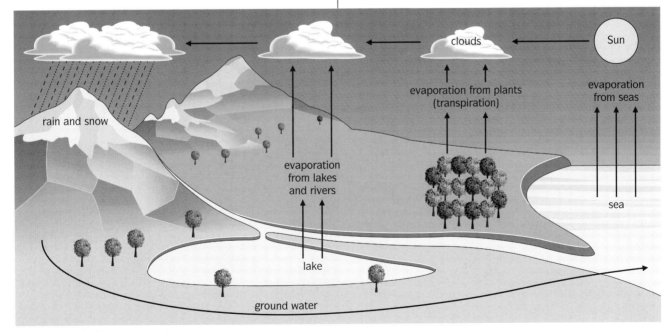

● *Figure 3.2* The water cycle.

rain that falls on land is returned to the atmosphere by evaporation and transpiration. The rest seeps through the soil and rocks, and flows by streams and rivers back to the sea.

The water in the cycle can dissolve or react with the various materials with which it comes into contact.

Sea-water	*(pH = 8.0)*	*River-water*	*(pH = 8.0)*	*Rain-water*	*(pH = 5.7)*
Cl^-	18980	HCO_3^-	58.4	Cl^-	3.79
Na^+	10540	Ca^{2+}	15.0	Na^+	1.98
SO_4^{2-}	2460	SO_4^{2-}	11.2	SO_4^{2-}	0.58
Mg^{2+}	1270	Cl^-	7.8	K^+	0.30
Ca^{2+}	400	Na^+	6.3	Mg^{2+}	0.27
K^+	380	Mg^{2+}	4.1	HCO_3^-	0.12
HCO_3^-	140	K^+	2.3	Ca^{2+}	0.09
Br^-	60	Fe^{2+}	0.67		

● **Table 3.1** Sample concentrations of ions in sea-water, river-water and rain-water, measured in $mg\,dm^{-3}$

Carbon dioxide dissolves in rain-water and attains an equilibrium with carbon dioxide in the surrounding air. Oxides of nitrogen and sulphur, both artificial and from natural sources, may also dissolve in the rain to produce nitric and sulphuric acids. We saw in chapter 2 that the principle artificial sources of nitrogen oxides in the atmosphere are emissions from vehicle exhausts, and that sulphur oxides mainly result from the combustion of fossil fuels. The acidic oxides dissolved in rain-water give it a pH value of between 5 and 6, although in 'acid rain' it may fall as low as 2 (chapter 2, page 16).

Rain-water will dissolve calcium-carbonate-based rocks:

$$CaCO_3(s) + CO_2(aq) + H_2O(l)$$
$$\longrightarrow Ca^{2+}(aq) + 2HCO_3^-(aq) \qquad (3.1)$$

and some silicate rocks:

$$Mg_2SiO_4(s) + 4H_2O(l)$$
$$\longrightarrow 2Mg(OH)_2(aq) + Si(OH)_4(aq) \qquad (3.2)$$
$$\Updownarrow$$
$$2Mg^{2+}(aq) + 4OH^-(aq)$$

The resulting ions make the water slightly alkaline, pH = 8, and are carried through the river system and into the oceans.

Natural waters

The dissolved species in typical samples of sea-water, river-water and rain-water are given in *table 3.1*. The composition of river-water can vary widely according to the types of rock that it, and its feeder streams, have passed over (*figure 3.3*).

Ions in the underlying rock will dissolve according to their solubility.

SAQ 3.1

Using *table 3.1*, compare Na^+, Ca^{2+}, Cl^- and HCO_3^- concentrations in sea- and river-water.

You can see that, although rivers run into the sea, there are pronounced differences between the composition of sea-water and that of river-water. It is interesting to note that the sodium ion, Na^+, is the most abundant metal ion in sea-water whereas the calcium ion, Ca^{2+}, is the most abundant in river-water. The reason for this is that the sodium ion has a very long residence time in the sea.

● *Figure 3.3*

A constant sodium ion balance is maintained by ion exchange with the clays in the sediment at the bottom of the sea:

$$Na^+(aq) + M\text{–}clay(s) \rightleftharpoons Na\text{–}clay(s) + M^+(aq)$$
$$(3.3)$$

The notation 'M–clay' means another cation, M, bonded to the silicate sheets present in clay. For a full discussion of the chemistry of clays, see chapter 5.

The concentration of potassium ions in natural waters is less than that of sodium ions because potassium is not as easily dissolved out of rocks, and is more readily removed from solution by forming complex ions with clays.

The magnesium and calcium ions in river-water come from the weathering of carbonate and silicate rocks. For example:

$$MgCO_3(s) + CO_2(aq) + H_2O(l)$$
$$\longrightarrow Mg^{2+}(aq) + 2HCO_3^-(aq) \qquad (3.4)$$

$$MgSiO_3(s) + 2CO_2(aq) + 3H_2O(l)$$
$$\longrightarrow Mg^{2+}(aq) + 2HCO_3^-(aq) + Si(OH)_4(aq)$$
$$(3.5)$$

Note that silicates can dissolve directly, as in *reaction 3.2*, and also in the presence of carbon dioxide, as in *reaction 3.5*. Some of the magnesium ions in sea-water are removed to form magnesium carbonate minerals. The formation of sea shells and corals reduces both the concentration of calcium ions in sea-water and that of the hydrogencarbonate ions, HCO_3^-.

The most abundant anion in sea-water is the chloride ion, Cl^-. Some of this comes from rocks and soils over which the water has passed before reaching the sea. The remainder comes from underwater volcanoes and vents in the seabed. Chlorine exists entirely as Cl^- and does not form stable complexes with any metal ions.

Carbon is present in natural waters as the carbonate ion, CO_3^{2-}, the hydrogencarbonate ion, HCO_3^-, and as dissolved carbon dioxide. The carbon dioxide comes from the air and decaying organic matter. Carbonate ions come from the weathering of carbonate rocks. The species CO_2, CO_3^{2-} and HCO_3^- are interchangeable depending upon the pH of the water. The equilibria are:

$$CO_2(aq) + H_2O(l) \rightleftharpoons H_2CO_3(aq) \qquad (3.6)$$

$$CO_2(aq) + H_2O(l)$$
$$\rightleftharpoons H^+(aq) + HCO_3^-(aq) \qquad (3.7)$$

$$HCO_3^-(aq) \rightleftharpoons H^+(aq) + CO_3^{2-}(aq) \qquad (3.8)$$

The species present at particular pH values are shown in *figure 3.4*.

The pH of natural water depends upon the amounts of dissolved CO_2, HCO_3^-, CO_3^{2-} and OH^-. The equilibria are *reaction 3.8* and:

$$HCO_3^-(aq) + H_2O(l)$$
$$\rightleftharpoons H_2CO_3(aq) + OH^-(aq) \qquad (3.9)$$

Solutions containing HCO_3^- are alkaline due to the predominance of OH^-.

In recent hot summers (1988/89/90) the algae content of some reservoirs has increased. These algae use dissolved carbon dioxide in photosynthesis causing the equilibrium

$$H_2CO_3(aq) \rightleftharpoons H_2O(l) + CO_2(aq) \qquad (3.10)$$

to move to the right. This removes H_2CO_3, so it moves *reaction 3.9* to the right, producing greater alkalinity in the water.

SAQ 3.2

Explain, using words and equations, why unpolluted river-water is alkaline.

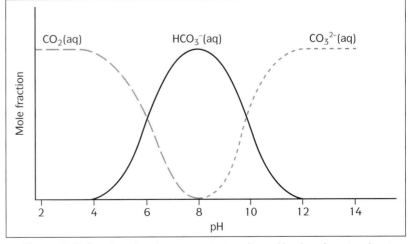

● *Figure 3.4* Species of carbon present at various pH values in natural water.

Chemistry at the water surface

At the water surface, or **air–water interface**, exchange of materials occurs between the atmosphere and the hydrosphere.

The amount of water vapour in the atmosphere is measured by relative humidity. This is expressed as:

$$\text{relative humidity} = \frac{\text{quantity of water in the air at } t\,^\circ C}{\text{maximum quantity air can hold at } t\,^\circ C}$$

$H_2O(l) \rightleftharpoons H_2O(g)$ moves to the right with increasing temperature. Fortunately, due to the continual movement of the atmosphere, liquid–vapour equilibrium is rarely attained, otherwise the high humidities attained would make life uncomfortable. High humidity is unpleasant, because the concentration of water molecules in the atmosphere makes it difficult for water to evaporate, so the process of sweating is impaired and the body cannot cool easily.

Solubility of gases

The solubility of gases in water can be found from Henry's Law, which states that the mass of gas, m, dissolved by a given volume of solvent is directly proportional to the pressure of the gas, p, provided the temperature remains constant and there is no reaction between the gas and solvent. This can be written as

$$m = kp$$

where k is Henry's law constant, which is different for each gas and is dependent upon temperature.

Vapour pressure

Think of a liquid in a closed container. Some of the molecules of the liquid will have enough energy to escape from the liquid and form a vapour above the liquid. These vapour molecules will collide with each other and with the walls of the container. Some will lose energy and return to the liquid. Eventually a state will be reached where the number of molecules leaving the liquid is equal to the number returning, provided the temperature remains constant. At this state the system is in dynamic equilibrium. The molecules in the vapour exert a pressure by bombarding the sides of the container. This pressure is known as the **vapour pressure** of the liquid.

If a **non-volatile** substance (a substance which does not easily vaporise) is dissolved in the liquid, the vapour pressure of the resulting solution is lower than that of the pure liquid. This occurs because part of the surface of the liquid is occupied by the non-volatile molecules, so fewer of the liquid molecules can escape.

Raoult's law relates the vapour pressure of a liquid in solution, $P(A)$, to its pure vapour pressure $P(A)^0$. It states that the relative lowering of the vapour pressure is equal to the mole fraction of the solute. The solute is the substance which dissolves in the liquid (the solvent).

The mole fraction of the solute is the number of moles of the solute, n_B, divided by the total number of moles of solute and solvent, $n_B + n_A$:

$$\text{mole fraction of solute} = \frac{n_B}{n_A + n_B}$$

So Raoult's law can be expressed mathematically as:

$$\frac{P(A)^0 - P(A)}{P(A)^0} = \frac{n_B}{n_A + n_B}$$

In the case we are considering, water is the solvent. Hence the presence of dissolved substances in natural waters will *lower* the vapour pressure.

Depression of freezing point

Solids also have a vapour pressure, although much less than that of liquids. The vapour pressure of both liquids and solids decreases as the temperature decreases. The temperature at which both the solid and liquid forms of a substance have the same vapour pressure is the melting or freezing point of that substance. It follows that if the vapour pressure of the liquid is lowered by the addition of a non-volatile solute, then the temperature at which the solid and liquid forms have the same vapour pressure will be less, and hence the melting point will be lower *(figure 3.5)*. Ice and water have the same vapour pressure at $0\,^\circ C$. In sea-water the presence of dissolved solutes reduces the freezing point to about $-2\,^\circ C$.

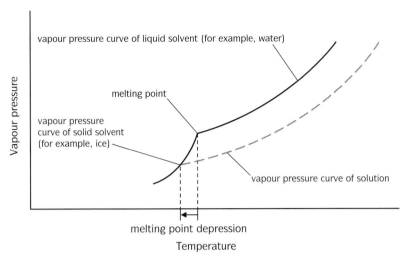

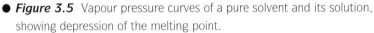

● **Figure 3.5** Vapour pressure curves of a pure solvent and its solution, showing depression of the melting point.

The importance of dissolved gases

The survival of aquatic life depends upon dissolved gases such as carbon dioxide and oxygen. Decaying organic matter causes a loss of oxygen which can have a serious effect upon fish life:

$$[CH_2O](aq) + O_2(aq) \longrightarrow CO_2(aq) + H_2O(l)$$
carbohydrate from
decaying organic matter

(3.11)

Assuming equilibrium between air and water, the amount of dissolved gas can be calculated.

Let us assume that normal atmospheric pressure is 101.3 kPa. The contribution towards this total pressure made by any particular gas is called the **partial pressure** of that gas.

The partial pressure of water vapour at 298 K = 3.2 kPa.

The fraction of oxygen in dry air is 0.209.

Therefore at 298 K the partial pressure of oxygen is given by:

$$p(O_2) = (101.3 - 3.2) \times 0.209 = 20.5 \, kPa$$

Henry's law constant for oxygen at 298 K
= $1.26 \times 10^{-5} \, mol \, dm^{-3} kPa^{-1}$

The concentration of dissolved oxygen is given by:

$$[O_2(aq)] = 1.26 \times 10^{-5} \times 20.5$$
$$= 2.58 \times 10^{-4} \, mol \, dm^{-3}$$
$$= 8.26 \, mg \, dm^{-3} \text{ since 1 mole oxygen has mass 32 g}$$

SAQ 3.3

Given that the fraction of nitrogen, N_2, in dry air is 0.79 and that the Henry's law constant for nitrogen at 298 K is $5.207 \times 10^{-6} mol \, dm^{-3} kPa^{-1}$, calculate the concentration (in $mg \, dm^{-3}$) of dissolved nitrogen in water at 298 K.

The chemistry of water

The water molecule forms part of a tetrahedral structure with two bonding electron pairs and two lone-pairs. The shared pair of electrons in the oxygen–hydrogen bond are polarised towards the oxygen, as it is more electronegative than the hydrogen.

Because lone-pairs are closer to the nucleus than bonding pairs, lone-pair–lone-pair repulsion > lone-pair–bonding pair repulsion > bonding pair–bonding pair repulsion. This leads to an H–O–H angle of 104.5°, which is less than the normal tetrahedral angle of 109.5°.

Polarisation of the O–H bond leads to electrostatic attraction between the hydrogen of one molecule and the lone-pair of another, which creates a hydrogen bond (*figure 3.6*). This relatively

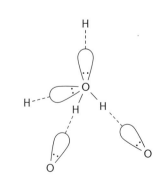

● **Figure 3.6** Hydrogen bonds between water molecules.

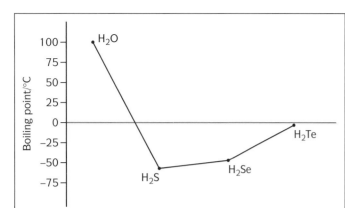

● **Figure 3.7** The variation of boiling point in the hydrides of Group VI.

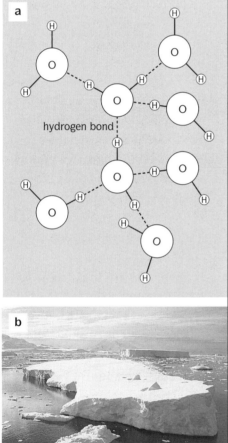

● **Figure 3.8**
a The structure of ice.
b Ice is less dense than water because of its open, hydrogen-bonded structure. Therefore, ice floats on water, as seen here in the Antarctic.

strong intermolecular bonding causes water to behave in a strange way. There is a wide range of temperatures (0–100 °C) for which water is a liquid, and its boiling point is much higher than other Group VI hydrides *(figure 3.7)*.

Ice has fully developed hydrogen bonding. The tetrahedral arrangement around each oxygen atom produces an open structure *(figure 3.8)* with a density less than that of water. Therefore ice will float on water.

The polar nature of water enables it to act as a good solvent, particularly for ionic species. But since there is strong interaction between water molecules, water will not act as a solvent for non-polar or very weakly polar solutes. However, for ionic solutes the ion–dipole attraction overcomes the interaction between the water molecules. *Table 3.2* shows that smaller ions have a greater attraction for water molecules, that is ions with the greatest charge density per unit of surface area have the greatest attraction. (The hydration number is the average number of water molecules held within the influence of a particular ion.)

For an ionic solid to dissolve, the process can be considered to occur in two stages:

■ The lattice is broken up into free 'gaseous' ions. The energy necessary to do this is equal to the reverse of the lattice energy (−LE). The **lattice energy** is the energy given out when 1 mole of a crystalline lattice is formed from its constituent ions in the gaseous state under standard conditions.

■ The individual ions are then hydrated with a sheath of water molecules. The energy change for this process is the enthalpy change of hydration.

So the enthalpy change of solution $\Delta H_{\text{solution}} = -\text{LE} + \Delta H_{\text{hydration}}$. The process may be represented by an energy cycle *(figure 3.9)*.

The enthalpy change of solution, $\Delta H_{\text{solution}}$, is often small in value compared with the values of lattice energy and enthalpy change of hydration. For a positive value of $\Delta H_{\text{solution}}$ the substance becomes more soluble as the temperature rises. For a negative value the opposite applies.

Ion	Ionic radius/nm	Charge density (charge/radius)	Hydration number	Hydration energy/ kJ mol^{-1}
Li$^+$	0.060	16.7	25.3	−498
Na$^+$	0.095	10.5	16.6	−393
K$^+$	0.133	7.5	10.5	−310
Rb$^+$	0.148	6.8	10.0	−284
Cs$^+$	0.169	5.9	9.9	−251

● **Table 3.2** Ions of Group I elements

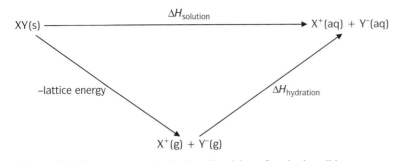

● **Figure 3.9** The energy cycle for the dissolving of an ionic solid.

Ionisation of water

Water is slightly ionised according to the equilibrium:

$$H_2O(l) \rightleftharpoons H^+(aq) + OH^-(aq) \qquad (3.12)$$

The **equilibrium constant**, K_c, for this equilibrium is expressed by:

$$K_c = \frac{[H^+(aq)][OH^-(aq)]}{[H_2O(l)]}$$

(Square brackets [ ] mean concentration of the species within the bracket expressed in $mol\,dm^{-3}$.)

Since $[H_2O(l)]$ is constant this is incorporated into K_c to give:

$$K_w = [H^+(aq)][OH^-(aq)]$$
$$= 10^{-14}\,mol^2\,dm^{-6} \text{ at } 298\,K$$

This is known as the **ionic product** of water.

For pure water, $[H^+(aq)] = [OH^-(aq)] = 10^{-7}\,mol\,dm^{-3}$. Therefore the pH value of pure water is 7. The pH of river-water and sea-water tends to be greater than 7 due to the presence of hydrogen carbonate ions (see pages 32 and 33).

Hydrolysis

Hydrolysis is the reaction of a substance with water. Metal ions tend to undergo solvation, followed by hydrolysis. As an O–H bond is broken, this leads to the formation of hydrogen ions and acidic solutions. For example:

$$Al^{3+}(aq) + 6H_2O(l) \rightleftharpoons [Al(H_2O)_6]^{3+}(aq) \qquad (3.13)$$

$$[Al(H_2O)_6]^{3+}(aq) \rightleftharpoons [Al(H_2O)_5OH]^{2+}(aq) + H^+(aq) \qquad (3.14)$$

Further dissociation occurs to give more hydrogen ions. Hydrolysis frequently stops when there is no charge on the metal species, in this case $Al(H_2O)_3(OH)_3$. This usually means that an insoluble product is formed. The hydrolysis of metal ions from Groups I and II tends not to proceed beyond the solvation stage.

The extent to which hydrolysis occurs depends on the polarising power of the metal cation. A small ion has a greater charge density than a larger one *(figure 3.10)*. The greater the number of charges for a similar surface area, the greater the charge density. You can see

same charge spread over larger surface area, therefore less charge density

● **Figure 3.10** Charge density on an ion.

that ions such as Be^{2+} and Al^{3+} would be expected to undergo extensive hydrolysis.

From *reaction 3.14* we would expect that the presence of an acid will suppress metal ion hydrolysis. This is because an increase in hydrogen ion concentration will move the reactions to the left. For this reason solutions of ions with a high charge density, such as Fe^{2+}, are made up in dilute sulphuric acid to stabilise them. For the metal hydroxides formed on hydrolysis, the higher the charge on the metal ion the lower the pH at which an insoluble hydroxide precipitates out as a solid *(table 3.3)*. Hence certain metal ions cannot exist as free ions in river-water and sea-water, which each have a pH of 8.

Ion	pH of precipitation as hydroxide
Mg^{2+}	10.0
Al^{3+}	9.8
Fe^{2+}	8.0
Ca^{2+}	6.5
Cu^{2+}	5.5
Cr^{3+}	4.1
Fe^{3+}	2.1
Ti^{4+}	1.2

● **Table 3.3**

Covalent compounds undergo hydrolysis by an attack upon an electrophilic centre by the lone-pair on the oxygen atom of water. Empty d-orbitals must be available to accommodate the lone-pair from the oxygen. For example:

$$SiCl_4(l) + H_2O(l) \longrightarrow SiO_2(s) + 4HCl(aq) \quad (3.15)$$

Metal oxides to the left of the Periodic Table are basic, and will react with water to form alkaline solutions.

Oxides of non-metals tend to be acidic, being hydrolysed by water to give an acidic solution. For example:

$$
\begin{aligned}
SO_2(aq) + H_2O(l) \\
\rightleftharpoons H_2SO_3(aq) \\
\rightleftharpoons H^+(aq) + HSO^{3-}(aq) \\
\rightleftharpoons SO_3^{2-}(aq) + 2H^+(aq) \quad (3.16)
\end{aligned}
$$

Oxides of elements in the middle of the table (for example aluminium, tin and lead) behave in both an acidic and a basic manner. We say they are **amphoteric**. For example:

■ aluminium oxide behaving as a base:

$$
\begin{aligned}
Al_2O_3(s) + 6HCl(aq) \\
\longrightarrow 2AlCl_3(aq) + 3H_2O(l) \quad (3.17)
\end{aligned}
$$

■ aluminium oxide behaving as an acid:

$$
\begin{aligned}
Al_2O_3(s) + 2NaOH(aq) \\
\longrightarrow 2NaAlO_2(aq) + H_2O(l) \quad (3.18)
\end{aligned}
$$

Hydrolysis is the final example of how water is a chemical with unusual properties which have a profound effect upon the geology and life of our planet. The water cycle shapes our weather patterns. The dissolving of oxygen and carbon dioxide, although it occurs in relatively small amounts, is essential to aquatic life. Hydrogen bonding in water is of fundamental importance to life processes, and the open structure of ice enables it to float on water – protecting aquatic life at the coldest temperatures. Water is indeed the life-blood of the Earth.

SUMMARY

■ The water cycle circulates water in the hydrosphere, lithosphere and atmosphere. It is important to the natural chemistry of the Earth.

■ Rain-water has a pH of between 5 and 6, due to dissolved carbon dioxide and the production of hydrogen ions by hydrolysis.

■ Natural water in streams and rivers is alkaline (pH = 8), due to the hydrolysis of hydrogen carbonate ions, HCO_3^-, which produces hydroxide ions, OH^-.

■ The laws of physical chemistry (for example Henry's law and Raoult's law) apply to the surface of water.

■ Water is an unusual chemical. Hydrogen bonding leads to unusual behaviour: high boiling point, ice floating on water, good solvent for polar solutes.

■ Water is slightly ionised. Ionic product $K_w = 1.0 \times 10^{-14} mol^2 dm^{-6}$.

■ Water solvates ions according to their size and charge.

■ Water reacts with some species through hydrolysis.

Questions

1 a Draw a dot-and-cross diagram to show the bonding in a water molecule.
   b (i) Explain, with the aid of a diagram, the interaction between adjacent water molecules.
     (ii) Indicate **two** important consequences that this interaction has on the physical properties of water.
   c What is meant by the statement that, at 25 °C, the ionic product for water is $1.0 \times 10^{-14} mol^2 dm^{-6}$?
   d Calculate the pH of pure water at 25 °C from the information given in **c**.
   e Explain why the pH of rain-water is approximately 5.7.

2 Give a brief account of the water cycle and explain why natural water tends to be alkaline.

Chapter four

Water pollution

(see page 44)

(see page 44)

(see page 44)

By the end of this chapter you should be able to:

1 discuss the different types of water pollution, their sources and their effects;

2 explain the meaning of *oxygen demand chemicals*;

3 discuss the movement of pollutants within the hydro-sphere;

4 describe the sources and effects of the major trace metals in water;

5 describe the main anionic pollutants and their effects;

6 explain the process of *eutrophication*;

7 explain the nature and causes of hardness of water, and methods for its removal.

Water pollutants can be roughly divided into seven types:

■ those containing organic materials which decay, reducing the amount of dissolved oxygen as they do so;

■ those which cause disease;

■ organic chemicals;

■ inorganic chemicals;

■ sediments;

■ nuclear waste;

■ those which warm water to a temperature that is unacceptable to aquatic life.

Organic materials which reduce the oxygen content of water as they decay are called **oxygen demand chemicals**. They are present in sewage from domestic waste and industrial sources. The food processing industry is particularly responsible for allowing this sort of material to enter the sewage system. Sewage and farm wastes can add to the eutrophication of water. **Eutrophication** is the process whereby water becomes over-rich in nutri-ents (see page 44). This also leads to a reduction in the level of dissolved oxygen in the water. Low oxygen levels in water are detrimental to normal aquatic life, such as fish species. The only species which survive are those especially adapted to low oxygen conditions.

Disease-causing pollutants are mainly carcino-genic (cancer causing) chemicals and microbes which cause disease, called pathogens. These tend to occur where there are uncontrolled wastes and high concentrations of people.

Organic chemicals such as pesticides, polychlori-nated biphenyls, petroleum wastes and detergents come from agricultural use and spillages. They can have an effect on all forms of life, depending upon their concentration. They can also cause eutrophi-cation.

Inorganic chemicals, trace elements, acids and bases come from industry and mining, and from the leaching of refuse dumps. They have effects on health, water quality and aquatic life. Sediments can have similar effects and in many cases come from the dumping of solid waste.

Nuclear power stations, the disposal of nuclear waste and mining in certain types of rock can lead to radionuclides in the water. These can also have implications for health.

Thermal pollution is a problem when water is used as a coolant in industrial heat exchangers and is then discharged into the water system. The steam used in power stations, to drive the turbines which generate electricity, is condensed and then cooled in high cooling towers. Even so it is still discharged into rivers and lakes at a temperature which causes thermal pollution. One effect of thermal pollution is that the solubility of oxygen in the water reduces as the temperature rises. This is detrimental to some forms of aquatic life. Warm water entering the surface layer of a lake can slow down the circulation of lake-water, which causes the water at the bottom of the lake to be low in dissolved oxygen (anaerobic) throughout the year. Warmer water encourages the growth of algae, which disrupt the normal ecological balance of the water system. Green algae flourish best at 30–35 °C and blue-green algae at 35–40 °C, as was seen in the hot summers in Britain in 1988/89/90.

Water in the environment is usually in motion, and therefore pollutants are usually moved around the hydrosphere and diluted. Pollutants can have effects at some considerable distance from the point where they entered the water system (*figure 4.1*). Occasionally pollutants are concentrated by feeding chains and other biological processes. Concentration of pollutants can also take place by chemical processes such as absorption, ion exchange and precipitation (*figure 4.2*).

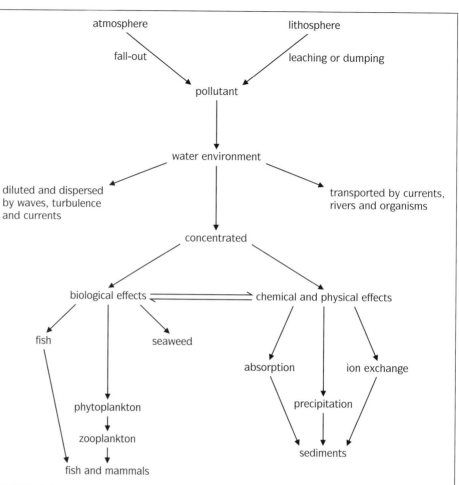

● **Figure 4.2** The movement of pollutants in the hydrosphere.

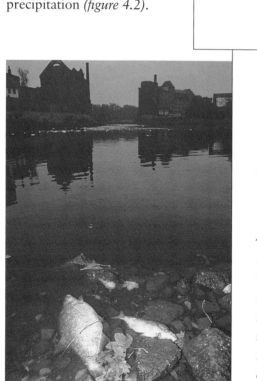

● **Figure 4.1** Pollution of rivers reduces the level of dissolved oxygen, causing damage to aquatic life. This is the river Elbe in Germany.

Metals

Even very small traces of metal in water can have a profound effect. The major trace metals in water that can be particularly harmful are mercury, lead, cadmium, arsenic, chromium and manganese.

Mercury

Mercury is considered to be the most dangerous of the metal pollutants. The major source of mercury pollution is in fact natural, most of this coming from degassing of the Earth's crust. Between 25 000 and 150 000 tonnes of mercury are released from the Earth's surface in this way every year. Human activity contributes about 20 000 tonnes a year (*table 4.1*) from fossil fuel combustion, cement manufacture and losses during industrial and agricultural processes. Mercury has been used to concentrate gold during the extraction process, sometimes resulting in cases of mercury poisoning and pollution of the environment. A process using activated charcoal is now eliminating this need for mercury.

Use	% total usage
electrolysis of brine to make NaOH and Cl₂	25
electrical switchgear	20
paints	15
instruments (thermometers, barometers)	10
catalysts	4
agriculture	5
dental fillings	3
pulp and paper manufacture	1
miscellaneous	17

● **Table 4.1** Uses of mercury

Mercury compounds are frequently used as catalysts in the manufacture of organic chemicals. For example:

$$C_2H_2(g) + H_2O(g) \xrightarrow{\text{HgSO}_4\text{(s)}} CH_3CHO(g) \qquad (4.1)$$
$$\text{ethanal}$$

$$C_2H_2(g) + HCl(g) \xrightarrow{\text{HgCl}_2\text{(s)}} CH_2{=}CHCl(g) \qquad (4.2)$$
$$\text{chloroethene}$$
$$\text{used to make PVC}$$

In agriculture, organo-mercury compounds are used as seed coatings to prevent the growth of fungi.

SAQ 4.2

Name the type of reaction that is taking place in *reactions 4.1* and *4.2*.

Localised concentrations of mercury pollution can have serious consequences for health. Mercury can cause serious damage to the nerves and brain which cannot be reversed. Mercury in water can be transformed by bacterial action into methylmercury, which is highly toxic. The process is outlined below.

$$Hg \xrightarrow[\text{O}_2 + \text{organics}]{} Hg^{2+} \xrightarrow[\substack{\text{(aerobic and anaerobic)}}]{\text{methane-producing bacteria}} CH_3Hg^+$$

Aerobic conditions apply in water, whereas anaerobic conditions are present in sediments. (Aerobic refers to an environment in which oxygen is present. Anaerobic refers to a lack of oxygen.)

Fish can carry methylmercury in their fat, which is dangerous to people who eat the fish. In 1953, 43 people died after eating fish from Minamata Bay in Japan. The mercury was discharged into the bay from a chemical plant where it had been used as a catalyst. More recently, in 1972 in Iraq 500 people died after eating flour made from grain that had been treated with methylmercury fungicide. Apart from those who died in these incidents, many more suffered irreversible brain damage. Symptoms of mercury poisoning are those resulting from damage to the nervous system: depression, irritability, paralysis, blindness and insanity.

Lead

Lead is a metal which is easily extracted from its ore and has many uses, for example in vehicle batteries, cable sheathing, lead sheeting and radiation shields.

Some older houses still have lead water pipes, from which lead can be dissolved at acidic pH. These pipes are dangerous where the water supply is drawn from a peaty area or contains a high level of carbonic acid. Cider and wine, which are acidic, should never be passed through lead pipes. Lead pipes are less of a danger in hard water areas.

Lead can enter the hydrosphere naturally from lead-bearing minerals in the Earth's crust, but it also enters from the refining and smelting process used in the extraction of lead, the use of lead pipes and other sources of industrial pollution. Lead can also enter the hydrosphere from glazed pottery that has been incorrectly fired and from the solder used in tin cans.

Acute lead poisoning is rare, requiring the ingestion of large quantities of lead salts. This is unlikely to occur in normal situations. The symptoms of acute lead poisoning are burning pains in the mouth, throat and stomach followed by severe abdominal pains and constipation or diarrhoea. In severe cases there is then failure of the kidneys, liver and heart, which leads to coma and death. Continual exposure to smaller concentrations of lead over a considerable period of time can lead to chronic lead poisoning. The symptoms appear gradually and are a general feeling of being unwell with vague pains in the abdomen and limbs. This sort of poisoning may arise from a high lead content in the water supply. There were some cases of this in rural districts of Scotland in the 1970s. Children are more susceptible to the effects of lead poisoning than adults, the main effect being upon the brain. Drowsiness, balancing difficulties, visual disturbances and mental retardation are the usual symptoms.

In mild cases of lead poisoning, the best treatment is simply to remove the patient from the source. The body may then eliminate lead by natural processes. In more severe cases lead may be removed from the body by chelating agents which encapsulate the lead ions. An example of a chelate is shown in *figure 4.3*.

Complex organic compounds such as edta (ethylenediaminetetra-acetic acid) have several lone-pairs of electrons in different parts of the molecule which can form a link with metal ions.

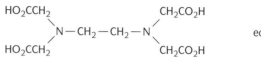

One molecule of edta forms six lone-pair links with a metal ion such as Pb^{2+}. Edta is therefore called a hexadentate ligand. In this way the lead ion is encapsulated and can be removed.

Cadmium

Cadmium is a highly toxic metal. A look at the Periodic Table will show that it is in the same sub-group as zinc, and hence it has similar physical and chemical properties. The similarities of atomic structure between cadmium and zinc allow cadmium to replace zinc in enzyme systems. For example, cadmium will replace zinc in carboxypeptidase, an enzyme which catalyses peptide degradation. Enzymes which contain cadmium do not work in biochemical situations.

Sources of cadmium in waterways are zinc mining areas, and uses such as metal plating and orange pigment in enamels and paints. Although cadmium compounds generally have low solubility, for example cadmium carbonate, in acidic solution the solubility is increased:

$$CdCO_3(s) + 2H^+(aq) \rightleftharpoons Cd^{2+}(aq) + CO_2(aq) + H_2O(l) \qquad (4.3)$$

In weakly alkaline situations the presence of dissolved carbonate will reduce the solubility of the cadmium ions, Cd^{2+}.

Since zinc and cadmium are similar, traces of cadmium are nearly always present wherever zinc is used. Hence corrosion of galvanised (zinc-coated) pipes and tanks adds cadmium to water. This can be reduced by pre-coating the metal to be galvanised with calcium carbonate or calcium metasilicate.

The recommended upper limit of cadmium in drinking water is 10 ppbv ($10 \mu g\,dm^{-3}$).

Arsenic

Arsenic is present in many different rocks. It occurs at concentrations of 1 ppm in limestone and silicous rocks, 2 ppm in igneous rocks, and up to 20 ppm in volcanic rocks. In the Wautapu Valley in New Zealand concentrations of up to 10 000 ppm have been recorded. It is frequently found with phosphate rocks and therefore

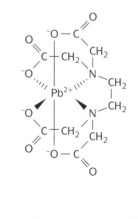

● **Figure 4.3** Edta chelation of lead ions.

occurs as an impurity in detergents and fertilisers. Contamination of water supplies by agricultural pesticides has occasionally been a source of arsenic poisoning. In Taiwan, natural water was found to contain 0.45% arsenic, and evidence of arsenic poisoning was shown by over 7000 villagers. Cement manufacture and waste from mining contribute further to the arsenic in the hydrosphere. It is interesting that the combustion of fossil fuels (mainly coal) contributes about 5000 tonnes of arsenic to the atmosphere each year. This is concentrated in aerosols and eventually precipitated back to the ground, where it accumulates in waterways.

Both oxidation states of arsenic are found in natural water. It occurs as the +3 state in AsO_2^- and AsO_3^{3-}, and as the +5 state in AsO_4^{3-}. The +5 state is the less toxic of the two. The normal levels of arsenic in natural water are about 2 ppbv. The recommended upper limit for drinking water is 50 ppbv.

Arsenic is concentrated in food chains and hence the eating of fish from contaminated areas can be dangerous. Arsenic in sediments can be methylated by bacterial action to produce the very toxic dimethylarsenic $(CH_3)_2As^+$.

The symptoms of chronic arsenic poisoning are general weakness, nausea and loss of appetite, followed by vomiting and diarrhoea. This leads to a well-known symptom of arsenic poisoning, peripheral neuritis. The nerves in the limbs cease to function properly, leading to tingling followed by loss of sensation to feet and hands. This loss of sensation creates difficulties in walking and other controlled movements.

Chromium

Chromium enters the waterways from mineral deposits, usually chromite, $FeO.Cr_2O_3$, and from its use in tanning and metal protection. Chromium(VI) is present in the ions $CrO_4^{2-}(aq)$ and $Cr_2O_7^{2-}(aq)$. It is toxic, but it is quickly reduced in aqueous solution to chromium(III), $Cr^{3+}(aq)$, by organic material. Chromium(III) shows very little toxicity.

Manganese

Manganese occurs in the oceans in nodules on the seabed. Typically, 20% of the manganese is in the form of manganese(IV) oxide, MnO_2. In acid conditions manganese occurs in water as $Mn^{2+}(aq)$ ions, but in alkaline conditions and an oxidising environment this is oxidised to manganese(IV) and precipitated as $MnO_2(s)$.

Dissolved oxygen

Although oxygen is relatively insoluble in water, dissolved oxygen is essential for aquatic life. As with most gases the dissolving of oxygen in water is an exothermic process and so, at a given pressure, the solubility decreases as the temperature increases. Solubility is also affected by the turbulence of the water, the concentration of dissolved salts, and the levels of bacterial, plant and animal life *(figure 4.4)*.

The lowest concentration of oxygen required for fish to survive is $3\,mg\,dm^{-3}$. Trout and salmon need higher concentrations. Organic material rapidly consumes dissolved oxygen with the help of microorganisms:

$$[CH_2O](aq) + O_2(g) \xrightarrow{microorganisms} CO_2(g) + H_2O(l)$$
$$\text{carbohydrate} \tag{4.4}$$

Another way of assessing the oxygen content of water is to measure the **biological oxygen demand**

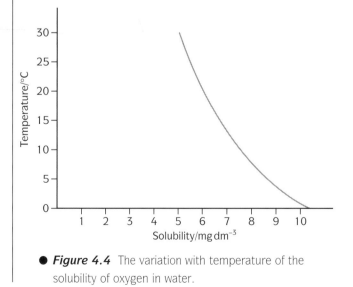

● *Figure 4.4* The variation with temperature of the solubility of oxygen in water.

(BOD). This is the amount of oxygen required by bacteria to achieve aerobic oxidation of organic material to carbon dioxide and water. To measure this, an experimental set-up is allowed to stand for five days and the oxygen level measured before and after.

The **chemical oxygen demand** (COD) measures the amount of material in the water that is oxidisable by chemical methods. There is a natural daily variation in the oxygen levels in water due to daytime photosynthesis and day- and night-time respiration. The level also varies as a consequence of added oxidisable pollutants that decrease the oxygen level. This level is normally restored naturally either after a certain period of time or, in a flowing waterway, further downstream. The time for the oxygen level to restore itself after the addition of a pollutant is called the **recovery time**. Recovery time depends upon the degree of agitation of the water. Greater agitation of the water will result in a larger surface area for air to dissolve in and hence quicker recovery. Therefore a fast-flowing river passing over rocks or waterfalls will restore its level of dissolved oxygen much quicker than a still lake or slow river.

When an organic pollutant enters a river or stream, the concentration of dissolved oxygen decreases due to the oxidation of the organic material by bacteria and protozoa. This is called the *zone of decline* or *decomposition zone*. Animal species such as leeches and snails can survive in this somewhat lower level of oxygen. Following this there is a zone where the level of dissolved oxygen is very low and relatively constant. This is the *damage* or *septic zone*. Here only a few species can survive, such as the sludgeworm and rat-tailed maggot. The level of oxygen then starts to increase again in the *recovery zone*, where the water starts to clear and sunlight may penetrate. Clean water is then restored. The curve of oxygen concentration produced by these processes is known as a **sag curve** and is shown in *figure 4.5*.

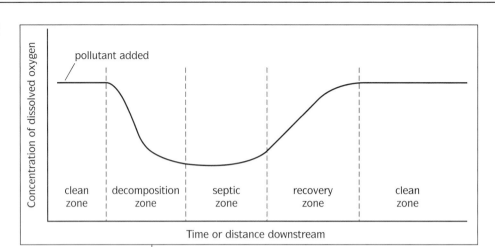

● *Figure 4.5* The variation of dissolved oxygen with time or distance downstream (sag curve).

Eutrophication

If too many nutrients enter, or are created in, a freshwater system, excessive plant and algal growth takes place. This is called eutrophication, and it makes the water cloudy and unsightly *(figure 4.6)*. When these plants and algae die and decay, dissolved oxygen is used up and parts of the water may become anaerobic, causing the formation of foul-smelling substances such as hydrogen sulphide, H_2S, ammonia, NH_3, and thioalcohols (alcohols in which the functional group contains sulphur instead of oxygen), RSH. Some of the

● *Figure 4.6* Algae clogging a ditch at Mildenhall, Suffolk, England. Standing water in this drainage ditch is completely covered with algae fed by nutrients lost from the fields.

nutrients are returned to the water when this happens. Rivers and streams purify themselves quickly, but lakes and static water can become marshy and eventually dry due to an accumulation of incompletely decomposed organic material.

Nitrates and, in particular, phosphates can cause excessive growth of algae. These substances enter freshwater systems from domestic, industrial and agricultural wastes. The use of phosphates in detergents has been a particular source of problems. Eutrophication can be controlled by the removal of phosphates from input waters. This is sometimes done by treating input waters with aluminium sulphate in sewage treatment plants; the phosphates are precipitated out as aluminium phosphate.

In summer, warm water can float on cold water, because the maximum density of water occurs at a temperature of 4°C. This is called **thermal stratification**, and it prevents the layers from mixing, so that dissolved oxygen in the top, warm layer does not pass to the colder, bottom layer. If there is a large amount of organic matter in the water, less sunlight will be able to penetrate, with a consequent reduction in photosynthesis and the production of oxygen. When the organic matter dies and decays, it falls into the lower layers and quickly uses up the dissolved oxygen, creating anaerobic conditions.

SAQ 4.3

Explain the meaning of the term 'eutrophication' in no more than **four** sentences.

Anionic species in water

The main anionic species are PO_4^{3-}, NO_3^-, SO_4^{2-} and CO_3^{2-}. Their concentrations affect the levels of dissolved oxygen and the growth of aquatic life. Sources are sewage effluent, industrial effluent, farm effluent, run-off from the land, drainage, leaf fall and bird droppings.

Phosphates always occur in the higher oxidation state, $+5$. In natural water with a pH of 8, the main species are $HPO_4^{2-}(aq)$ and $H_2PO_4^-(aq)$. Polyphosphates from detergents undergo

hydrolysis to give $HPO_4^{2-}(aq)$:

$$P_3O_{10}^{5-}(aq) + 2H_2O(l)$$
$$\rightleftharpoons 3HPO_4^{2-}(aq) + H^+(aq) \qquad (4.5)$$

The HPO_4^{2-} forms salts which are not very soluble. These end up in sediments or are adsorbed onto clays.

Nitrates are more soluble than phosphates and readily leach from soils into watercourses. The denitrifying bacteria which normally remove nitrates from water are unable to cope with the extra nitrate from the land. The recommended level of nitrate(V), NO_3^-, in drinking water is $10\,mg\,dm^{-3}$. The EU legal limit is $50\,mg\,dm^{-3}$. This is frequently breached in most EU countries.

In very young children nitrate(V) may be reduced to nitrate(III), NO_2^-, by bacteria in the stomach. Young children do not have sufficient acid in their stomachs to prevent the growth of these bacteria. Sometimes this leads to a fatal condition called blue baby syndrome in which nitrate(III) oxidises the iron(II) in haemoglobin to iron(III).

Cyanide from metal cleaning, electroplating and gold extraction sometimes escapes into water systems. It is hydrolysed in water to produce hydrogen cyanide, HCN, which is a weak acid:

$$CN^-(aq) + H_2O(l)$$
$$\rightleftharpoons HCN(aq) + OH^-(aq) \qquad (4.6)$$

Since hydrogen cyanide is volatile, the equilibrium in *reaction 4.6* is shifted to the right. Cyanide is highly poisonous as it bonds irreversibly with iron(III), preventing its reduction to iron(II) in cells.

The hardness of water

Hard water is a nuisance in many areas. It is difficult to produce a good lather with soap when using hard water. A white scum is produced instead, which collects in the fibres of clothes and around the edges of sinks and baths. Hard water also leads to the furring up of kettles, boilers and pipes. On the other hand, hard water helps create strong teeth and bones, and the incidence of heart disease is lower in hard-water areas.

The hardness is due to dissolved calcium and magnesium ions. These ions find their way into the natural water supply because of the action of dissolved carbon dioxide on carbonate rocks:

$$CaCO_3(s) + H_2O(l) + CO_2(aq)$$
$$\underset{\text{limestone}}{} \rightleftharpoons Ca^{2+}(aq) + 2HCO_3^-(aq) \qquad (4.7)$$

$$\underset{\text{dolomite}}{CaCO_3.MgCO_3(s)} + 2H_2O(l) + 2CO_2(aq)$$
$$\rightleftharpoons Ca^{2+}(aq) + Mg^{2+}(aq) + 4HCO_3^-(aq) \ (4.8)$$

If it is considered necessary to remove the hardness in water, it can be done by one of three methods. The method chosen is the one most appropriate to the situation.

■ **Removal of Ca^{2+} and Mg^{2+} as insoluble precipitates.** This can be achieved by boiling the water:

$$Ca^{2+}(aq) + 2HCO_3^-(aq)$$
$$\longrightarrow CaCO_3(s) + H_2O(l) + CO_2(g) \qquad (4.9)$$

or adding washing soda, $Na_2CO_3.10H_2O$:

$$Ca^{2+}(aq) + Na_2CO_3(aq)$$
$$\longrightarrow CaCO_3(s) + 2Na^+(aq) \qquad (4.10)$$

or adding slaked lime, $Ca(OH)_2$:

$$Ca^{2+}(aq) + HCO_3^-(aq) + OH^-(aq)$$
$$\longrightarrow CaCO_3(s) + H_2O(l) \qquad (4.11)$$

■ **The formation of soluble complexes.** In detergent products, polyphosphates, $P_3O_{10}^{5-}$, are used to soften water, resulting in the formation of soluble complexes with magnesium and calcium ions:

$$Ca^{2+}(aq) + P_3O_{10}^{5-}(aq)$$
$$\longrightarrow \underset{\text{soluble}}{CaP_3O_{10}^{3-}(aq)} \qquad (4.12)$$

The detergent molecules themselves can also act as softening agents (R is a long hydrocarbon chain):

$$2ROSO_3^-Na^+(aq) + Ca^{2+}(aq)$$
$$\longrightarrow \underset{\text{soluble}}{(ROSO_3)_2Ca(aq)} + 2Na^+(aq) \qquad (4.13)$$

■ **Using ion exchange resins:**

$$resin-H_2(s) + Ca^{2+}(aq)$$
$$\longrightarrow resin-Ca(s) + 2H^+(aq) \qquad (4.14)$$

Water supply

A **potable** water supply is one which is drinkable. It must be free of pathogens (disease-causing organisms), have no undesirable tastes, odours, colours or turbidity, and contain no harmful organic or inorganic chemicals. Natural water often has to be treated to make it potable (*figure 4.7*).

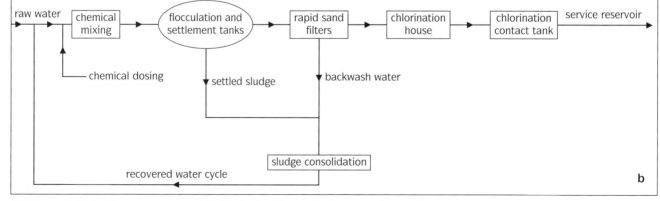

● *Figure 4.7* **a** Water treatment at Mythe Water Works, Tewkesbury, England.
b Layout of typical water treatment plant for public supply.

It would be difficult, and expensive, to isolate and identify all the possible disease-causing organisms in a water supply. Tests have been devised that estimate the level of bacterial contamination by the 'coliform count', which is a measure of the number of *Escherichia coli* bacteria per cubic centimetre. This bacterium rarely causes disease, but its presence in water indicates the likely presence of other disease-causing organisms. As *Escherichia coli* occurs naturally in the intestines of warm-blooded animals, its presence in a water supply suggests faecal pollution. Directives from the European Union and the World Health Organization require *Escherichia coli* to be absent from public water supplies. It should not be detectable in $100 \, cm^3$ of water.

If the water is stored, 50% of the pathogens die within 2 days and 90% within 7 days. Chemical treatment is necessary to remove other pathogens. Storage also allows large particles to separate out on standing. This is called **sedimentation**.

Unpleasant taste, odour and colour can be caused by algae in the supply reservoirs. The water is aerated to remove hydrogen sulphide, carbon dioxide, methane and any other volatile material. Aeration also removes odorous bacteria and oxidises any iron(II) and manganese(II) present.

If hardness is considered to be a problem, calcium ions and magnesium ions are removed in the form of insoluble carbonates by the addition of washing soda and slaked lime (lime-soda). The high pH of this process also precipitates Fe^{3+} as iron(III) hydroxide, $Fe(OH)_3(s)$, and any manganese ions as manganese(IV) oxide, $MnO_2(s)$.

Natural waters frequently contain particles which, though solid, are supported by the liquid, so that there is very little tendency for the particles to separate out. These particles are called **colloids** and are too small to be visible with an ordinary microscope. Their size is generally in the range 1×10^{-9} to $1 \times 10^{-7} \, m$. Colloids and other fine materials are precipitated by adding aluminium sulphate. The Al^{3+} ions hydrolyse to give a gelatinous (jelly-like) hydroxide precipitate, which absorbs other ions and solids as it settles. This practice is being reviewed in Britain following the accident at Camelford in

Cornwall in 1990, when aluminium sulphate was accidentally tipped into the wrong tank resulting in high levels of aluminium in the local water supply, and because of concern about the effect of aluminium on health.

Aluminium is toxic to all forms of life: plant and animal. In humans, there is a strong link between aluminium and Alzheimer's disease, which results in a loss of memory and other mental faculties particularly in the elderly. The maximum admissible concentration of aluminium in drinking water, as specified in the EU drinking water directive of 1985, is $200 \, \mu g \, dm^{-3}$.

Harmful bacteria are killed by the addition of chlorine. Chlorine reacts with water to form chloric(I) acid, HClO (hypochlorous acid):

$$Cl_2(aq) + H_2O(l) \rightleftharpoons H^+(aq) + Cl^-(aq) + HClO(aq) \qquad (4.15)$$

This reacts further to give the chlorate(I) (hypochlorite) ion:

$$HClO(aq) + H_2O(l) \rightleftharpoons H_3O^+(aq) + ClO^-(aq) \qquad (4.16)$$

Chloric(I) acid and chlorate(I) ions kill bacteria by oxidation. Chlorate(I) is sometimes added directly to water as sodium chlorate(I) or calcium chlorate(I). It is important that the oxidation effect is maintained during the distribution stage of water supply, as well as at the water treatment and storage plant. This is achieved by the addition of ammonia which produces chloroamines:

$$NH_3(aq) + HClO(aq) \longrightarrow NH_2Cl(aq) + H_2O(l) \qquad (4.17)$$

$$NH_2Cl(aq) + HClO(aq) \longrightarrow NHCl_2(aq) + H_2O(l) \qquad (4.18)$$

$$NHCl_2(aq) + HClO(aq) \longrightarrow NCl_3(aq) + H_2O(l) \qquad (4.19)$$

The reaction of the chloroamines with water in the distribution system gradually releases chlorate(I) ions, which kill bacteria.

A problem with water chlorination is the production of chlorinated organic matter, such as trichloroalkanes (haloforms), from the low-concentration organic pollutants which remain in water. Ozone is an effective alternative to chlorine, and its use is becoming more widespread.

Organic chemicals, such as pesticides and trichloroalkanes, are removed by passing the water through a filter of granular carbon. The European Union has set very strict limits on the pesticide content of drinking water. The limit is 1 part of pesticide in 10 000 million parts of water (0.1 ppbv). That is the equivalent of one drop in a full-sized swimming pool!

In some countries where eutrophication is a problem, there is an additional process which removes phosphate(V) ions by precipitation using aluminium ions, iron(III) ions and the addition of lime. If removal of nitrate(V) is necessary, it is achieved by specialised populations of bacteria working in anaerobic conditions, which convert nitrate to nitrogen gas and water.

The treatment of sewage

The treatment of sewage at any one location depends upon the type of sewage and its contents, and upon the pollution regulations at that location *(figure 4.8)*.

● *Figure 4.8* A typical rural sewage works. Secondary treatment takes place in the round areas, which contain a bed of small stones over which the sewage water trickles. A slime growing on the rocks contains microorganisms that remove organic material from the sewage water.

The first job in sewage treatment is to remove paper, rag, wood and other rubbish which would cause blockages or damage machinery. This is done by screens (closely spaced metal bars), or a device which chops up the rubbish. Grit and silt can also damage the system, so this is removed by a detritor or grit channel. If the sewage passes through this channel at the right speed, the grit will settle whilst the lighter liquid will carry on. Sometimes hydro-cyclone grit traps are used, in which a fast revolving system separates the grit by centripetal forces. In this type of system, the sewage flow is switched off periodically to allow the grit chamber to be washed out, all automatically. There are usually stormwater weirs to cope with heavy rain. High flows pass over the weirs and are passed to storage tanks until the storm subsides.

Primary treatment of sewage removes solid materials by sedimentation. The fine solid impurities suspended in the liquid gradually settle to the bottom of the holding tanks, where they are removed in the form of a liquid sludge. Any scum forming at this stage is removed by a device which skims the scum from the surface of the water. The remaining sewage water flows over weirs and on for further treatment. Some of the material removed is oxidisable, so this lowers the BOD and COD levels. Up to 60% of suspended solids can be removed in this way.

Secondary treatment removes dangerous bacterial and organic material that, if released into rivers, would increase oxygen demand in waterways. No chemicals are used. Sewage from the primary stage is sprayed over beds of small stones coated with natural microorganisms and other small life-forms such as worms and flies. Given sufficient air, this colony will feed on the organic material in the sewage, oxidising it to carbon dioxide, water and nitrogen compounds. The nutrients nitrogen and phosphorus are necessary for this process.

In a newer method of secondary treatment the bacteria and sewage are stirred up to form 'activated sludge'. Air is forced into the sludge and this aeration encourages the microorganisms to multiply. The aeration also encourages them to feed on and oxidise the organic material in the sewage. The organic nitrogen and phosphorus are released as nitrate(V) and phosphate(V) ions.

The primary and secondary treatments together remove approximately 90% BOD, 80–90% COD, 90% suspended solids, up to 50% nitrogen, 30% phosphorus and some dissolved materials.

The activated sludge solids must be removed from the treated effluent, and this happens in a final settlement stage. Some of the activated sludge is recycled to the previous stage in order to return some of the microorganisms to the aeration tank. Any very fine solids remaining are removed by a polishing treatment. This is done by sand filtration, or by microstraining in which the effluent passes through rotary screens with very fine mesh.

Sometimes, particularly in small rural communities, the effluent is allowed to stand in wide, shallow ponds called lagoons. After this the effluent can be discharged to a watercourse.

Sludge from primary and secondary treatments is pumped to 'dewatering' tanks, where it thickens on standing, and the top water is pumped back to the inlet to go through the whole treatment process again. The thickened sludge is heated in a closed tank or digester and kept at 35 °C for about 20 days. In the digester, bacteria convert organic matter into methane (which can be used to heat the digester), and the sludge is changed from an objectionable state to a creamy black sludge that smells like tar. A centrifuge turns the sludge into a 'cake' which is delivered to local farmland for use as a soil conditioner and fertiliser.

The main sewage treatment processes are summarised in *table 4.2*.

SAQ 4.4

Explain the problems caused by the release of nitrate and phosphate to river waters (refer to pages 44 and 45).

SUMMARY

■ The types of water pollution are:
  • oxygen-demanding;
  • disease-causing;
  • chemical – organic and inorganic;
  • sediments;
  • nuclear waste;
  • warm water.

■ Pollutants move around the hydrosphere.

■ Very small traces of metal can be harmful pollutants.

■ Dissolved oxygen is essential to aquatic life. The oxygen content of water is measured by the biological oxygen demand (BOD) and the chemical oxygen demand (COD).

■ Eutrophication occurs when too many nutrients enrich a freshwater system, causing excessive growth of algae and other aquatic plants. Decay of these uses up oxygen, leading to anaerobic conditions.

■ The main anionic pollutants are phosphates and nitrates.

■ Hardness of water is due to dissolved calcium and magnesium ions.

■ To obtain water that is drinkable, natural water undergoes a series of physical, chemical and biological processes.

■ Sewage is treated to enable the waste waters to be discharged safely into rivers and the sea.

Process	Type of treatment	Basic purpose
preliminary	screening and grit removal	removal of large abrasive solids
primary treatment	settlement in tanks	removal of solids and grease
secondary treatment	activated sludge, percolating filter, other biological treatment, plus settlement	bio-oxidation of organic matter and ammonia, and removal of solids
polishing treatment	sand filtration and micro-straining or lagooning	removal of very fine solids
tertiary treatment	denitrification and chemical precipitation	removal of nitrogen, phosphorus and organic residuals
sludge treatment	digestion, thickening, dewatering and drying	methane production and preparation for disposal

● *Table 4.2* Summary of main sewage treatment processes

Questions

1 Make a table summarising the main trace metal pollutants in water, giving their sources and effects.

2 **a** Identify an ion that, when present in water, causes the water to be hard.
  b Explain why its presence prevents the ready formation of a lather with soap.
  c State **two** ways in which the hardness of water may be removed.

3 State **three** methods used to analyse water samples. Give full experimental details of one such analysis that you have carried out yourself.

Chapter five

The lithosphere

By the end of this chapter you should be able to:

1 explain the nature of the lithosphere in terms of igneous, sedimentary and metamorphic rocks;

2 discuss the composition of soils in terms of sand, silt and clay content using a soil texture chart;

3 explain the ion-exchange capacity of soils and the variation in soil pH;

4 discuss chemical weathering of the landscape in terms of chemical principles such as lattice and hydration energies and hydrolysis.

● **Figure 5.1** Fingal's Cave on the island of Staffa off the west coast of Scotland, showing columnar basalt.

Most of the lithosphere is composed of rocks and clays which are made of silicates and aluminosilicates. Because the Si–O bond energy is high at $468\,kJ\,mol^{-1}$, silicates are resistant to chemical attack. Silicates therefore resist weathering and persist in the environment. In aluminosilicates some silicon atoms are replaced by aluminium atoms. These aluminosilicates are the basis of feldspars and clays.

Types of rock

The rocks of the Earth are of three kinds: igneous, sedimentary and metamorphic.

Igneous rocks

Igneous rocks are made from cooled liquid magma from beneath the Earth's crust. They are of two types: intrusive and extrusive.

Intrusive igneous rocks are formed from magma that has cooled slowly beneath the surface of the Earth, so these rocks consist of large crystals. Granite is the most common intrusive igneous rock. It has large crystalline grains of mica, quartz and feldspar, and contains 73% silicon dioxide by mass. As it is formed at great depths, granite is only exposed where ancient earth movements have lifted the rocks. Thus granite is found in the highlands of Britain, for example in the Scottish Highlands and the Dartmoor tors.

Extrusive igneous rocks have cooled rapidly on the Earth's surface, often from magma emitted from volcanoes, and they therefore consist of small crystals. Basalt is a common extrusive igneous rock and contains on average 52% of silicon dioxide by mass. Basalt may form hexagonal columns, as at the Giant's Causeway in Northern Ireland and Fingal's Cave on the island of Staffa off the west coast of Scotland (figure 5.1).

Sedimentary rocks

The formation of sedimentary rocks starts with the weathering of other rocks by sun, wind, rain, frost and chemical processes. The broken-up material is transported, mainly by water, and deposited in rivers, lakes and the sea in the form of loose sediments.

The loose sediments settle out onto the river bed or the seabed and are cemented together with minerals such as silica, SiO_2, calcite, $CaCO_3$, dolomite, $CaCO_3.MgCO_3$, gypsum, $CaSO_4.2H_2O$, anhydrite, $CaSO_4$, and iron oxides. They are compressed by the pressure of overlying material into various kinds of sedimentary rock.

■ Oolitic limestone (figure 5.2) contains very small chalky spheres cemented together. It has a creamy colour and is used as a building stone.

● *Figure 5.2* Oolitic limestone with fossils.

■ Chalk *(figure 5.3)* is a pure form of limestone: brilliant white when freshly exposed, fine grained and permeable. It often contains flints and fossils.

● *Figure 5.3* Chalk.

■ Sandstone *(figure 5.4)* is composed of small, rounded quartz granules which appear glassy. These granules are cemented together with feldspar minerals. The red and brown sandstones derive their colour from iron oxides.

● *Figure 5.4* Sandstone.

■ Conglomerates are composed of rounded pebbles from many different types of rock cemented together by silica or calcite.

Sandstone and conglomerate are examples of clastic sedimentary rocks, that is they are formed from fragments of rocks.

Metamorphic rocks

When rocks are heated and/or compressed inside the Earth they recrystallise while still remaining solid to form metamorphic rocks *(figure 5.5)*. New minerals frequently form in this process.

The compression results in these minerals being lined up in the same direction: such rocks are said to be foliated. Examples are slate, schist and gneiss. Slate splits into thin sheets along planes (called cleavage planes). Schist is a medium- to coarse-grained rock in which mica grains can easily be seen lined up in the same plane. Quartz and feldspar are the other minerals present in schist. Gneiss is coarse-grained with obvious banding.

Hornfels is a metamorphic rock formed by heat alone. The rock is unfoliated and the minerals are not lined up.

Some metamorphic rocks are described in *table 5.1*.

During metamorphism, new mineral groupings are produced which depend on the pressure and temperature when the new rocks were formed. Important metamorphic minerals are muscovite mica, $KAl_2(AlSi_3O_{10})(OH)_2$, biotite mica, $K(Mg,Fe)_5(Al,Fe^{3+})_2Si_3O_{10}(OH)_8$, pyroxenes, for example $NaAlSi_2O_6$, and the garnets, for example $Ca_3Cr_2(SiO_4)_3$.

● *Figure 5.5* Metamorphic rock showing the layer structure.

Name	Original rock	Cause of formation	Minerals contained	Grain size
marble	limestone	heat	calcite	medium
metaquartzite	sandstone	heat	quartz	medium
schist	mudstone	heat and pressure	mica, quartz, feldspar, garnet	medium to coarse
gneiss	mudstone	heat and pressure	mica, quartz, feldspar, hornblende	medium to coarse
slate	mudstone	pressure	mica, quartz, feldspar	very fine
hornfels	mudstone	heat	quartz, feldspar, pyroxene	fine to medium

● **Table 5.1** Metamorphic rocks

	Igneous	Sedimentary	Metamorphic
Grain type	crystalline	fragmental	crystalline
Grain direction	not usually lined up	not usually lined up	usually lined up
Fossils	absent	may be present	absent
Appearance when broken	shiny, glassy	usually dull	shiny
Ease of breaking	hard, not easily split	may be soft and crumbly	hard, may split into layers

● **Table 5.2** Identification of rock type from examination of specimens

Table 5.2 shows how you can identify a rock sample.

Soil

From a chemist's viewpoint, soil is a mixture of inorganic and organic materials with particle sizes ranging from colloids (see chapter 4, page 47) to small stones. It contains water and gases in variable proportions and, of course, some living material.

The principal inorganic constituents of soil are sand, silt and clay in varying proportions. Soil texture is determined by the relative proportions of these constituents in the soil *(figure 5.6)*.

■ Sand is mainly quartz, SiO_2, of particle size 0.05–2.0 mm (fine sand 0.05–0.1 mm, coarse sand 1.0–2.0 mm). Sandy soils are light and easy to dig, but because of the relatively large particle size they allow water to pass through easily. Thus soluble mineral salts are easily leached from sandy soils.

■ Silt is again mainly quartz plus other silicates, but with particles of a much smaller size (0.002–0.05 mm).

■ Clay particles have diameters of less than 0.002 mm and consist of silicate and aluminosilicate minerals.

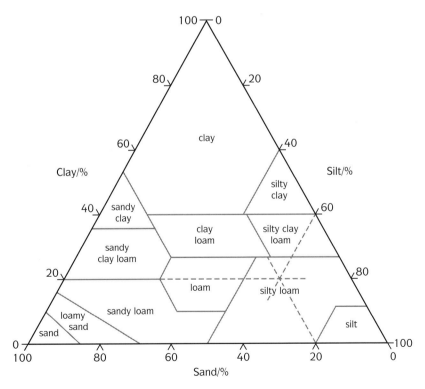

● **Figure 5.6** Soil texture chart. The example, marked with dashed lines, consists of 60% silt, 20% sand and 20% clay; it is a silty loam.

The movement of water and gases through the soil is related to the amount and size of spaces between the particles. This is determined in part by the average particle size, which depends upon the proportions of sand, silt and clay in the soil.

Clay has the smallest particles, therefore the number of spaces between the particles is greatest in a given volume. These spaces are small enough to produce capillary action, which draws water into the clay. Clay therefore has a greater water-holding capacity than sandy soil, but much of this water is bound to minerals or is contained in microscopic pores and is therefore unavailable to plants. Sandy soils have a low water-holding capacity, but most of the water is available to plants.

The water in soil contains dissolved minerals that act as nutrients for plants. The amount and composition of the dissolved nutrients depends on the pH of the soil solution, so acidic and basic pollutants can affect the nutrient composition of the water in soil.

The air in soil has a similar composition to that in the troposphere, but it is richer in carbon dioxide because of decay processes. Normally the physical and chemical conditions favour oxidation, which helps in the decay of organic material, but in a waterlogged soil reduction can occur, leading to a change in the products of the decomposition of organic matter. In reducing conditions, anaerobic bacteria predominate, and the products of decomposition are volatile carboxylic acids and ethene instead of carbon dioxide.

Layer silicates

Clays have a layered structure. There are three basic types of clay, known as 1:1, 2:1 and 2:2. These ratios refer to the arrangement of the two different sheet structures in the clay. One sheet consists of SiO_4^{4-} tetrahedra with three corners shared (*figure 5.7*). The oxygen atoms at the fourth corners of the tetrahedra (all these corners point in the same direction) are also involved with the

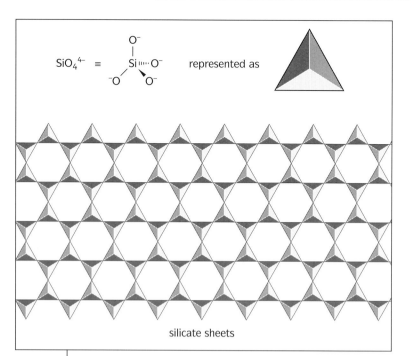

● **Figure 5.7** Silicate ions are able to form a silicate sheet by sharing three corners with other silicate ions.

second sheet. Some of the silicon atoms in the first sheet may be substituted, in varying amounts, by aluminium.

SAQ 5.1
Draw a dot-and-cross diagram of the silicate ion.

The second sheet is made up of close-packed oxygen atoms and hydroxyl groups arranged as octahedra, with aluminium, or sometimes magnesium, in the octahedral holes – the metal atom is surrounded by six oxygen atoms.

Clays contain both kinds of sheets, either in the ratio of one tetrahedral sheet to one octahedral sheet, known as a 1:1 clay, or two tetrahedral sheets to one octahedral sheet, known as a 2:1 clay. A 2:2 clay is similar to a 2:1 clay, but it contains an extra second sheet in which some of the aluminium atoms are replaced by iron and magnesium atoms.

Kaolinite is a 1:1 clay (*figure 5.8*). There is one tetrahedral sheet and one octahedral sheet in each layer, the layers being held together by hydrogen bonding. Water cannot enter between the layers because of the hydrogen bonding, so kaolinite does

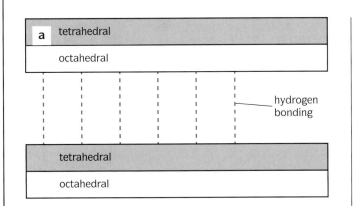

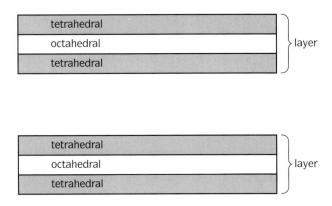

• *Figure 5.9* 2:1 clay.

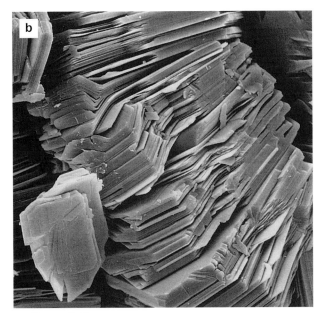

• *Figure 5.8*

a 1:1 clay.

b Photomicrograph of kaolinite showing the layer structure.

not expand when wet. The relatively weak nature of hydrogen bonding means kaolinite can be easily broken up between the fingers. These properties make kaolinite suitable for use as modelling clay.

Examples of 2:1 clays are vermiculite and montmorillonite *(figure 5.9)*. In this arrangement there is little attraction between the silicate oxygens of the tetrahedral sheets in different layers, so water and cations can enter the space between the layers. This water forces the layers apart, exposing a large internal surface area and causing the clay to expand when wet. This makes soils containing 2:1 clays difficult to plough and dig. When these soils dry the opposite effect takes place and the soil shrinks and cracks *(figure 5.10)*.

In 2:1 clays, some aluminium ions in the octahedral sheet are substituted by magnesium ions, which leaves individual layers with a high negative charge. Vermiculite also has one quarter of the silicon(IV) atoms replaced by aluminium(III) ions, so the negative charge is greater still. The large surface area of these clays with a high negative charge attracts cations that are hydrated *(figure 5.11)*, which gives the wet clay a sticky feel. These cations can also be exchanged with other cations contained in the surrounding soil solution. This property of 2:1 clays, known as the permanent cation-exchange capacity, is an important feature in the retention of cationic nutrients and their supply to plants.

An example of a 2:2 clay is chlorite.

SAQ 5.2

Explain why the addition of aluminium ions causes clay particles to flocculate. (A 'floc' is a feathery precipitate. When such a precipitate settles out the process is called **flocculation**.)

• *Figure 5.10* Dried-out, cracked 2:1 clay.

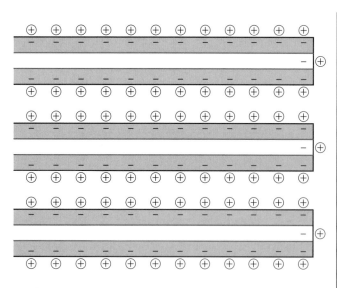

● *Figure 5.11* Cations at the surface of a 2 : 1 clay.

Organic matter

Organic matter in soil can be divided into non-humic and humic types.

■ Non-humic material is the undecomposed or partly decomposed fragments of plants and soil organisms.

■ Humic material is called humus, and is a complex mixture of brown amorphous and colloidal substances modified from the original plant and animal tissue by microorganisms. The compounds it contains are highly polymerised.

As humus forms, the cellulose material is broken down but the protein is retained. Humus influences the water-holding capacity of a soil, its ion-exchange capacity and the binding of metal ions. Lone-pairs of electrons on the nitrogen atoms of long protein molecules are able to donate into empty orbitals on metal ions, forming a ring structure called a chelate.

In this way, essential metal micronutrients are held in the soil by the humus and are prevented from being leached out. They are slowly released in the process of ion exchange, and are taken up by plants through their roots.

The properties of soil

Ion-exchange capacity and soil pH are inter-related and influence the availability of plant nutrients. Pollutants can affect both of these properties.

Ion-exchange capacity

The ion-exchange capacity of a soil means its ability to hold and exchange ions.

Clays have a large surface area and are therefore good ion exchangers. As explained earlier, clays containing aluminium are permanently anionic and are able to hold hydrated cations, M^+, at their surface:

$$clay^-(s) + M^+(aq) \longrightarrow clay–M(s) \qquad (5.1)$$

These cations can be replaced by different ions from the soil solution in a process called cation exchange:

$$clay–M(s) + M'^+(aq) \rightleftharpoons clay–M'(s) + M^+(aq) \qquad (5.2)$$

These cation-exchange properties are permanent as a result of ion exchange within the mineral.

The cation-exchange capacity of a clay mineral is measured as the number of moles of exchangeable positive charge held by 1 kg of the mineral. Typical values are $1.5 \, mol \, kg^{-1}$ for vermiculite, $1.0 \, mol \, kg^{-1}$ for montmorillonite and $0.3 \, mol \, kg^{-1}$ for kaolinite.

The surface of a clay consists of layers of oxides and hydroxides. At high pH the hydroxyl group loses protons, or the protons are replaced by metal ions:

$$clay–OH(s) \rightleftharpoons clay–O^-(s) + H^+(aq) \qquad (5.3)$$

$$clay–OH(s) + M^+(aq) \rightleftharpoons clay–OM(s) + H^+(aq) \qquad (5.4)$$

Similarly organic acids in soils can act as cation exchangers:

$$R–C\!\!\begin{array}{c}O\\\\OH\end{array}(s) + M^+(aq) \rightleftharpoons R–C\!\!\begin{array}{c}O\\\\OM\end{array}(s) + H^+(aq) \qquad (5.5)$$

These ion-exchange processes are important in plant nutrition *(figure 5.12)*. For example, if potassium ions are taken out of solution by plants, clays release potassium ions from clay–K back into the solution to re-establish equilibrium – the clay acting as a reservoir of nutrient cations. Some herbicides, such as paraquat and simazine, may affect this process, because they are adsorbed onto the surface of the soil particles, even though they are said to become 'inactive' in the soil.

Clays also have an anion-exchange capacity:

$$\text{clay–OH(s)} + \text{A}^-\text{(aq)}$$
$$\rightleftharpoons \text{clay–A(s)} + \text{OH}^-\text{(aq)} \qquad (5.6)$$

● **Figure 5.12** A vine leaf grown **a** with and **b** without the nutrient potassium.

Nitrate ions are only held weakly, and are easily washed out, so clay soils are not good retainers of the nitrate nutrient, NO_3^-. Phosphate, PO_4^{3-}, is strongly held, especially in clays with high aluminium and iron content. This means that much of the phosphate added to clay soil becomes bonded to the clay and is not available to plants. As a class experiment you may wish to investigate the ion-exchange properties of some soils.

Soil pH

The pH of a solution is a measure of its acidity or alkalinity. It is defined as the negative logarithm of the hydrogen ion concentration:

$$\text{pH} = -\log_{10}[\text{H}^+\text{(aq)}]$$

Soil pH is a very important factor in plant growth and normally ranges from 3 to 9. Large amounts of humus in the soil induce acidity, since humus contains a high proportion of carboxylic acid groups. This may be counterbalanced if high concentrations of basic cations are present. A pH close to 7 in soils is associated with large amounts of exchangeable calcium.

Acidity can also be induced by the presence of significant quantities of aluminium in solution. This generally comes from the weathering of rocks and clays. A lower pH encourages this weathering process:

$$\text{Al}_2\text{Si}_2\text{O}_5(\text{OH})_4(\text{s}) + 6\text{H}^+\text{(aq)}$$
$$\underset{\text{kaolinite}}{}$$
$$\longrightarrow 2\text{Al}^{3+}\text{(aq)} + 2[\text{Si(OH)}_4](\text{s}) + \text{H}_2\text{O(l)} \; (5.7)$$

As the aluminium ion has a high charge density, it complexes with water and then regenerates hydrogen ions:

$$[\text{Al(H}_2\text{O)}_6]^{3+}\text{(aq)}$$
$$\longrightarrow [\text{Al(OH)(H}_2\text{O)}_5]^{2+}\text{(aq)} + \text{H}^+\text{(aq)}$$
$$\longrightarrow [\text{Al(OH)}_2(\text{H}_2\text{O)}_4]^+\text{(aq)} + 2\text{H}^+\text{(aq)}$$
$$(5.8)$$

Aluminium ions adhere strongly to exchange sites on clays because of their high charge, and they maintain the local acidity as a result of *reaction 5.8*.

Cations adsorbed onto the surface of clays affect the pH when they are released.

■ For example, the pH is raised by:

clay–Na(s) + H_2O(l)
$\rightleftharpoons$ clay–H(s) + Na^+(aq) + OH^-(aq) (5.9)

■ The pH is lowered by:

clay–Al(s) + $4H_2O$(l)
$\rightleftharpoons$ clay–H_3(s) + $Al(OH)_4{}^-$(aq) + H^+(aq)
(5.10)

If a soil has a high proportion of its cation-exchange sites occupied by hydrogen ions, it will not be able to supply plants with the nutrients they need.

In an acid medium, nitrate ions, $NO_3{}^-$(aq), may be reduced to ammonium ions, $NH_4{}^+$(aq):

$NO_3{}^-$(aq) + $10H^+$(aq) + $8e^-$
$\longrightarrow NH_4{}^+$(aq) + $3H_2O$(l)   (5.11)

Plants are usually only able to accept nutrients in an oxidised form, hence increased acidity of the soil reduces the availability of nitrogen for plant growth. To maintain nitrogen in an oxidised form, a well-aerated soil is necessary to provide a sufficient supply of oxygen to enable the reverse of *reaction 5.11* to take place. An acidic soil encourages the solubility of toxic metal ions such as mercury, cadmium and lead, whose effects have been discussed in chapter 4.

The effect of soil pH on the availability of nutrients is shown in *table 5.3*.

Points to note from *table 5.3*:

■ Calcium and magnesium are removed from soil solution at high pH because they form insoluble carbonates.
■ Little iron, manganese or aluminium is found in solution above pH 6 because of the formation of insoluble hydroxides.
■ At a low pH, nitrogen is less available as a nutrient because of the reduction of nitrate to ammonium.
■ The availability of the nutrient phosphate is greatest at a pH of between 6 and 7. This is because the most soluble form of phosphate is $H_2PO_4{}^-$ which exists over the pH range 2–7. However, below pH 6 insoluble iron and aluminium phosphates form, and above pH 7 insoluble $Ca_3(PO_4)_2$ forms.

Therefore to ensure the best conditions for available nutrients the soil pH needs to be carefully controlled. Soil pH is controlled by natural systems to a certain extent. The equilibria present when carbon dioxide dissolves in water were mentioned in chapter 3. Hydrogen carbonate ions, $HCO_3{}^-$(aq), can remove some of the hydrogen ions, thus acting as a buffer:

$HCO_3{}^-$(aq) + H^+(aq) $\rightleftharpoons H_2CO_3$(aq)
$\rightleftharpoons CO_2$(g) + H_2O(l)   (5.12)

However, you will recall from *figure 3.4* (page 33) that below pH 4.5 there are virtually no hydrogen-

Nutrients	pH								
	3	4	5	6	7	8	9	10	11
calcium magnesium	maximum availability						form insoluble carbonates		
iron manganese aluminium	maximum availability				form insoluble hydroxides				
phosphorus	forms insoluble iron and aluminium phosphates				maximum availability		forms insoluble calcium phosphate		
nitrogen sulphur					maximum availability				
potassium					maximum availability				
copper zinc				maximum availability					

● *Table 5.3* Effect of soil pH on the availability of nutrients

carbonate ions, so therefore there is a limit to this buffering action. Humus also has a buffering action as it contains organic acids:

$$RCO_2^-(s) + 2H^+(aq) \rightleftharpoons RCO_2H(s) + H^+(aq)$$
$$\rightleftharpoons RCO_2H_2^+(s) \qquad (5.13)$$

Artificial increase in soil pH is achieved by liming the ground using calcium carbonate (limestone) or calcium hydroxide *(figure 5.13)*. This is usually done once every five to ten years as the liming material is only lost relatively slowly from the soil by leaching because of its low solubility. *Table 5.4* gives the lime requirements of various soils. Liming works as follows:

$$clay-H_2(s) + CaCO_3(s)$$
$$\longrightarrow clay-Ca(s) + H_2O(l) + CO_2(g) \qquad (5.14)$$

$$clay-Ca(s) + 2H_2O(l)$$
$$\rightleftharpoons clay-H_2(s) + Ca^{2+}(aq) + 2OH^-(aq) (5.15)$$

● *Figure 5.13* Spreading lime on ploughed hill pasture in Shropshire, England, prior to grass sowing. Liming of soils increases their pH.

Sometimes the efficacy of liming is affected by 'acid surges' after the melting of ice and snow that was formed from acidified water. These surges involve a rapid release into the soil of a large quantity of acidic water, which a previous liming may be unable to neutralise.

On the rare occasions when it is necessary to lower soil pH, this is done by adding acid salts such as ammonium sulphate:

$$NH_4^+(aq) \rightleftharpoons NH_3(aq) + H^+(aq) \qquad (5.16)$$
$$clay^-(s) + H^+(aq) \rightleftharpoons clay-H(s) \qquad (5.17)$$

You may wish to do experiments on the determination of soil pH and the determination of the lime requirement of a soil.

SAQ 5.3

A soil of pH 5.5 is composed of 40% sand, 30% silt and 30% clay. Calculate the amount of lime required, in tonnes per hectare.

Chemical weathering

Weathering is the breaking-down of rocks and rock surfaces by the action of water, oxygen and carbon dioxide. The chemical processes of weathering are dissolving, hydration, carbonation, hydrolysis, oxidation and reduction.

Dissolving and hydration

The most common soluble ionic materials in the Earth's crust are sodium chloride (solubility $350\,g\,dm^{-3}$) and calcium sulphate (gypsum and

pH	Loamy sands	Sandy loams	Loams Silty loams Silt loams Organic sandy loams	Clay loams Organic loams Silt loams Peat loams	Clays Organic clay loams Peat
6.0	20	25	30	40	50
5.5	40	50	65	80	100
5.0	60	75	95	120	150
4.5	80	95	130	160	190
4.0	100	120	160	200	240
3.5	120	145	190	245	290

● *Table 5.4* Lime requirements of various soils (measured in tonnes per hectare)

anhydrite, $2\,g\,dm^{-3}$). Silica ($6.5 \times 10^{-3}\,g\,dm^{-3}$) is slightly soluble:

$$SiO_2(s) + 2H_2O(l) \rightleftharpoons H_4SiO_4(aq) \qquad (5.18)$$
$$\text{silicic acid}$$

The solubility of ionic solids can be explained in terms of their lattice energy and the enthalpy change of hydration of their ions.

■ The enthalpy change of hydration, ΔH_{hyd}, is the energy given out per mole on the solvation of gaseous ions by water molecules:

$$M^{x+}(g) + nH_2O(l) \longrightarrow [M(H_2O)_n]^{x+}(aq) \qquad (5.19)$$

The enthalpy change of hydration decreases in size with increasing ionic radius *(figure 5.14)*, because the surface charge density reduces as the ionic size increases. The enthalpy change of hydration increases in size with increasing ionic charge *(figure 5.15)*, because the surface charge density increases as the ionic charge increases.

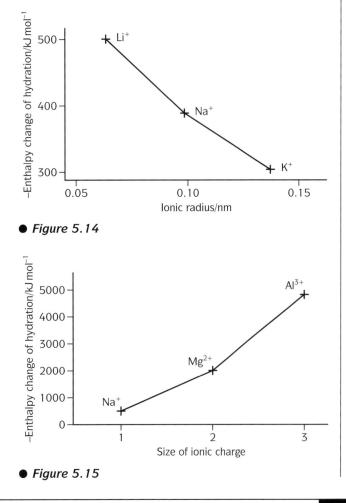

● *Figure 5.14*

● *Figure 5.15*

■ The lattice energy, ΔH_{latt}, is the energy given out when 1 mole of an ionic lattice is formed from its gaseous ions.
■ The enthalpy change of solution, ΔH_{soln}, is the enthalpy change when 1 mole of solute dissolves to form an infinitely dilute solution.

These three quantities are related by:

$$\Delta H_{soln} = -\Delta H_{latt} + \Delta H_{hyd} \qquad \text{(see page 36)}$$

Hence the lattice energy and the enthalpy change of hydration work against each other.

The most soluble ions have a low charge and a large radius, for example Cs^+, Rb^+ and K^+.

Ions with a high charge and a small radius may hydrolyse in water to give insoluble hydroxides. For example:

$$Al^{3+}(aq) + 3H_2O(l) \rightleftharpoons Al(OH)_3(s) + 3H^+(aq) \qquad (5.20)$$

The high charge density of the aluminium weakens one of the O–H bonds.

The solubility of many minerals is dependent on pH. For example, the solubility of silicon dioxide is increased by a higher pH because the equilibrium moves to the right:

$$H_4SiO_4(aq) + H_2O(l) \rightleftharpoons H_3O^+(aq) + H_3SiO_4^-(aq) \qquad (5.21)$$

Carbonation

The reaction of carbon dioxide dissolved in water with materials in the Earth's crust is referred to as carbonation. Carbon dioxide reacts with water to form an acidic solution (chapter 3, page 33):

$$CO_2(g) + H_2O(l) \rightleftharpoons H^+(aq) + HCO_3^-(aq) \qquad (5.22)$$

This reacts further with minerals such as calcium carbonate:

$$CaCO_3(s) + H^+(aq) \rightleftharpoons Ca^{2+}(aq) + HCO_3^-(aq) \qquad (5.23)$$

The overall reaction may be written as:

$$CaCO_3(s) + CO_2(g) + H_2O(l) \rightleftharpoons Ca^{2+}(aq) + 2HCO_3^-(aq) \qquad (5.24)$$

● **Figure 5.16** Limestone pavement showing clints and grykes in the Yorkshire Dales, England.

This reaction causes rapid weathering of calcium carbonate minerals. Limestone caves and the grykes found on limestone pavements are an example of this reaction *(figure 5.16)*. Sometimes so much limestone dissolves and collapses that a deep vertical sink hole or swallow hole is formed. A well-known example is Gaping Ghyll near Ingleborough in the Yorkshire Dales, England, which is 120 metres deep.

When water drips from a cave roof, carbon dioxide is lost to the air, the reverse of *reaction 5.24* takes place and minute amounts of solid calcium carbonate form. These build up to form stalactites hanging from the roof. A similar process takes place when the water drop hits the floor, causing stalagmites to grow upwards *(figure 5.17)*.

When water rich in dissolved calcium carbonate is aerated, for instance at waterfalls, carbon dioxide is again lost and calcium carbonate is deposited as tufa.

Limestone areas which have their landforms produced mainly by carbonation (and the reverse reaction) are said to have karst landscapes, as in the Yorkshire Dales, England.

Hydrolysis

Hydrolysis is the reaction of water with some other species leading to the breaking of an O–H bond, and the formation of an acidic or alkaline solution.

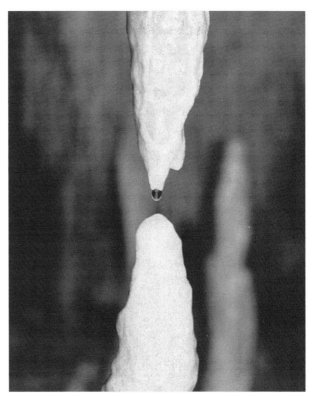

● **Figure 5.17** Stalactites and stalagmites. This stalactite (growing down) has almost met the stalagmite (growing up), which has been formed from the same drops of water.

■ An example of formation of an acidic solution is:

$$SO_2(g) + H_2O(l) \rightleftharpoons 2H^+(aq) + SO_3^{2-}(aq)$$
$$(5.25)$$

■ An example of formation of an alkaline solution is:

$$CaO(s) + H_2O(l) \rightleftharpoons Ca(OH)_2(aq) \qquad (5.26)$$

Hydrolytic weathering of minerals occurs by the breaking of an O–H bond and also possibly an M–O bond (M is a metal atom). The minerals with the weakest M–O bonds weather first and are most easily removed from the rock. The bond energies of some M–O bonds are as follows, in $kJ\,mol^{-1}$.

Ti–O	674
Al–O	582
Si–O	464
Ca–O	423
Mn–O	389
Fe–O	389
Mg–O	377

SUMMARY

- There are three kinds of rock: igneous, sedimentary and metamorphic.

- Soils are a mixture of sand, silt and clay in various proportions according to the type of soil.

- Humus is decomposed organic material present in soil.

- Soil can act as an ion-exchange agent.

- Soil pH varies considerably. It needs to be controlled to obtain the best conditions for the available nutrients.

- Rocks are broken down by reactions with water and air.

- Hydrolysis and carbonation are the main chemical processes in the weathering of rocks.

Questions

1 a Describe the nature of igneous sedimentary and metamorphic rocks, mentioning observations that you have made. Explain their origins.

  b Discuss the physical and chemical weathering of rocks, giving equations where possible.

  c Particles of rock, mixed with partly decomposed plant debris (humus), form soil.
Explain the function of chelating agents in the humus. What happens to soil particles when acid rain falls on them?

2 a Give the **two** main groups of rocks in the Earth's crust other than igneous rocks.

  b Explain how you could distinguish between these **three** groups of rocks from observations of hand specimens and thin sections.

  c Describe a chemical test that may be used to distinguish limestone from an igneous rock.

  d Explain how you could distinguish between extrusive and intrusive igneous rocks.

  e Outline **two** processes that occur when a rock is exposed to chemical weathering.

  f Name a region of the world where you would expect chemical weathering to be particularly rapid. Give a reason for your answer.

The motor car is an example of a product in which a complex range of materials has been used in its construction. Scrapyards *(figure 6.8)* sell second-hand spare parts and this is an example of re-using, which is more efficient than recycling. Copper from electric motors and radiators is recovered, as is lead from batteries and cast iron from the engine block. Cars are being developed which are made from recyclable metals. For example, some cars have an aluminium body which the manufacturers claim is 70% recyclable.

Hazardous and toxic wastes

The safe disposal of hazardous and toxic wastes is a specialised and growing industry. Pyrolysis (heating to a high temperature in the absence of oxygen) is generally used, but no useful products can be recovered from this except thermal energy.

Many industries are required by law to treat their wastes before discharge to watercourses or sewage works. In the case of wastes containing unacceptable levels of heavy metal ions, this can be done by ion exchange. For example, a resin containing suitable anions (with attached sodium cations) can be used to extract the heavy-metal cations:

$$\text{resin}\begin{smallmatrix} X^-\ Na^+ \\ \\ X^-\ Na^+ \end{smallmatrix}\text{(s)} + M^{2+}\text{(aq)} \longrightarrow \text{resin}\begin{smallmatrix} X^- \\ \\ X^- \end{smallmatrix}M^{2+}\text{(s)} + 2Na^+\text{(aq)}$$

(6.3)

The sodium ions released are less harmful than heavy metals in the environment. The resin becomes exhausted after a period of time and can be regenerated by treatment with dilute sulphuric acid followed by aqueous sodium hydroxide. Sometimes the heavy metals can be recovered for re-use.

Radioactive waste

Spent fuel rods from nuclear reactors are processed to separate out fission products including uranium and plutonium. The rods are first dissolved in nitric acid to give nitrate salts of the fission products. Uranium and plutonium are separated from the other fission products by mixing the solution with an organic solvent, immiscible with water, which selectively dissolves these elements. Repeated mixing with fresh solvent, and removal of the solvent layer, transfers almost all the uranium and plutonium to the solvent. This process is called **solvent extraction**.

Some fission products have a long half-life (the time taken for the intensity of radiation to fall to half its original value), which creates storage and disposal problems. Initially, they are stored in solution in cooled tanks. Storage as a glass is better because of the smaller bulk.

There are many suggestions for ultimate storage, including deep-sea trenches, old mine shafts and injection into rocks. All suggestions to date have drawbacks.

SAQ 6.2

Explain how the process of solvent extraction can be used to separate a mixture.

SUMMARY

■ The heavy metals cadmium, copper and zinc are the chief pollutants of soil, together with organic pesticide residues.

■ Lead present in urban dusts is of particular environmental concern.

■ Solid wastes are disposed of by dumping, sanitary landfill, incineration, dumping at sea or recycling.

■ Satisfactory methods for the disposal of radioactive waste have not yet been found.

Questions

1 a A sanitary landfill is a means of waste handling that is much less disruptive to the environment than uncontrolled dumping either on land or in the ocean.
Describe how such a landfill should be managed and mention particularly the chemical problems associated with such a waste-handling scheme.

  b Incineration is a means of disposing of municipal waste that is being used increasingly in some countries.
Discuss the advantages and disadvantages of this means of disposal.

  c Discuss another procedure for dealing with some wastes that is environmentally favourable.

2 a (i) Describe **two** types of soil pollutant.

  (ii) Explain why organic pollutants tend to remain in the top layer of soil and are not generally leached in to water courses. Why is it that some organic pollutants do manage to reach water courses?

  b Explain the nature of urban street dust. How does it arise? Explain how the profile of urban street dust varies with distance from the road edge and with soil depth.

Answers to self-assessment questions

Chapter 1

1.1 Chlorophyll absorbs at 660–680 nm (red) and 425–430 nm (blue) and reflects in the green area.

1.2 Increased carbon dioxide concentration and a damp atmosphere, together with a temperature of about 15–20 °C and artificial radiation of about 680 nm and 430 nm.

1.3 Photosynthesis is rapid in rainforests. This removes excess carbon dioxide from the atmosphere and helps maintain a balance. Removal of rainforests will lead to an increase in atmospheric carbon dioxide and hence global warming.

1.4 Nitrogen is reduced to ammonia which is used in the biosynthesis of amino acids. These are essential for making plant proteins.

Green chlorophyll is a nitrogen-based, complex organic chemical. A lack of nitrogen will thus prohibit the synthesis of chlorophyll and lead to yellowing of leaves. Lack of chlorophyll will result in less photosynthesis and stunted growth.

1.5 Reactions following the absorption of radiation are exothermic, for example:

$$O^* + O_2 + M \longrightarrow O_3 + M^*;$$
$$\Delta H = -100\,kJ\,mol^{-1}$$

$$O_3 + O \longrightarrow 2O_2;$$
$$\Delta H = -390\,kJ\,mol^{-1}$$

$$H\cdot + O_3 \longrightarrow \cdot OH + O_2;$$
$$\Delta H = -326\,kJ\,mol^{-1}$$

1.6 Production:

$$O_2 \xrightarrow{hf} O + O^*$$
$$O^* + O_2 + M \longrightarrow O_3 + M^*$$

Removal:

$$O_3 \xrightarrow{hf} O_2 + O$$
$$O_3 + O \longrightarrow 2O_2$$
$$NO\cdot + O_3 \longrightarrow NO_2\cdot + O_2$$
$$H\cdot + O_3 \longrightarrow \cdot OH + O_2$$

1.7 These reactions in the thermosphere absorb ultraviolet radiation:

$$O_2 \xrightarrow{hf} O + O$$
$$O_2 \xrightarrow{hf} O_2^+ + e^-$$

Chapter 2

2.1 Denitrification. Denitrifying bacteria reduce nitrate(V):

$$NO_3^-(aq) \longrightarrow NO_2^-(aq) \longrightarrow NO(g)$$
$$\longrightarrow N_2O(g) \longrightarrow N_2(g)$$

2.2 $2.41 \times 10^{-7}\,m = 241\,nm$

2.3 $3.53 \times 10^{-7}\,m = 353\,nm$

2.4 $C + O_2 \longrightarrow CO_2$
$6 \times 44/12 = 22$ billion tonnes (assume complete combustion)

2.5 Just above tropopause by:

$$\cdot OH + CO \longrightarrow CO_2 + H\cdot$$

Soil bacteria and fungi:

$$CO + \tfrac{1}{2}O_2 \longrightarrow CO_2$$
$$4CO + 2H_2O \longrightarrow CH_4 + 3CO_2$$

Reaction of oxygen atoms:

$$CO + O + M \longrightarrow CO_2 + M$$

Conversion by plant leaves:

$$CO \longrightarrow \text{amino acids in daylight}$$

$$CO \longrightarrow CO_2 \text{ at night}$$

Reasons why these equations do not work in cities:
hydroxyl radical does not exist at street level due to lack of light;
few soil bacteria or fungi;
few plant leaves.

2.6 CaCO$_3$:
$$\text{molar volume} = \frac{100}{2.71}$$
$$= 36.9\,\text{cm}^3$$

CaSO$_4$:
$$\text{molar volume} = \frac{136}{2.96}$$
$$= 45.9\,\text{cm}^3$$

CaSO$_4$.2H$_2$O:
$$\text{molar volume} = \frac{172}{2.32}$$
$$= 74.1\,\text{cm}^3$$

Both forms of calcium sulphate have a greater molar volume than calcium carbonate. Therefore, if calcium sulphate replaces calcium carbonate in a crack in stonework it will force the crack apart, creating stress forces in the stonework.

2.7 The number of deaths closely follows smoke and sulphur dioxide levels. The highest sulphur dioxide and smoke levels follow several days of low temperature. Particulates aggravate the effect of sulphur dioxide, which affects heart and lung function and causes severe respiratory distress *(table 2.4)*.

2.8 See *figure*.

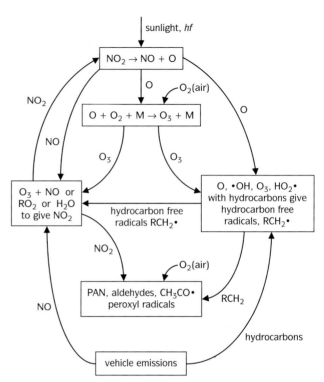

● *Answer for* SAQ 2.8

2.9 Nitrogen monoxide is emitted from cars in the morning rush hour. At first this is slowly oxidised to nitrogen dioxide, the concentration of which peaks about two hours later than that of nitrogen monoxide because of the absence of an effective oxidising agent. Full daylight splits up nitrogen dioxide, releasing oxygen atoms. These react with oxygen molecules in the presence of particulate matter from car exhausts to form ozone, which builds to a peak concentration in the early afternoon. Nitrogen monoxide formed later in the day removes the ozone to reform oxygen molecules. The nitrogen dioxide formed does not undergo further photolysis as there is little light in the evening rush hour.

2.10 2-Methylbuta-1,3-diene.

2.11 A secondary pollutant is one which is formed by the chemical reactions of emitted pollutants.

Emission of nitrogen oxides and particulates is restricted by use of catalytic converters in motor vehicles and higher air : fuel ratio to ensure more complete combustion. Smoke emission can be stopped or electrostatic precipitators can be used to eliminate it.

2.12 Lack of reactivity.

2.13
$$CCl_2F_2 \xrightarrow{hf} \cdot CClF_2 + Cl\cdot$$
$$Cl\cdot + O_3 \longrightarrow ClO\cdot + O_2$$
$$ClO\cdot + NO\cdot \longrightarrow Cl\cdot + NO_2\cdot$$
$$ClO\cdot + NO_2\cdot \longrightarrow ClNO_2 + O$$
$$ClO\cdot + O \longrightarrow Cl\cdot + O_2$$

Chapter 3

3.1 The concentration of each of the ions is higher in sea-water than in river-water. In sea-water the concentration of Na^+ is greater than that of Ca^{2+}, whereas in river-water the concentration of Ca^{2+} is greater than that of Na^+.

Cl^- is the most abundant ion in sea-water, whereas it has relatively low abundance in river-water.

HCO_3^- is the most abundant ion in river-water, but has relatively low abundance in sea-water.

In sea-water the concentration of Cl^- is much greater than that of HCO_3^-, but in river-water the position is reversed.

3.2 *Figure 3.4* shows the hydrogencarbonate ion, HCO_3^-, to be the dominant acid–base species in natural water at pH range 6–10.

The equilibrium for HCO_3^-(aq) acting as an acid:

$$HCO_3^-(aq) \rightleftharpoons H^+(aq) + CO_3^{2-}(aq)$$

favours the left-hand side more than the equilibrium for HCO_3^-(aq) acting as a base:

$$HCO_3^-(aq) + H_2O(l) \rightleftharpoons H_2CO_3(aq) + OH^-(aq)$$

Therefore the solution will have a greater concentration of OH^-(aq) than H^+(aq) and will be alkaline.

3.3 $p(N_2) = (101.3 - 3.2) \times 0.79 = 77.5\,kPa$

$[N_2(aq)] = 5.207 \times 10^{-6} \times 77.5$
$= 4.036 \times 10^{-4}\,mol\,dm^{-3}$
$= 11.3\,mg\,dm^{-3}$ (1 mol N_2 has a mass of 28 g)

Chapter 4

4.1 Water pollutants – see *table*.

Type of pollutant	Sources	Effects
oxygen-demanding sewage	domestic and industrial waste food processing	reduced oxygen levels in water eutrophication
disease-causing chemical carcinogens and pathogens	uncontrolled wastes crowded urban environment	effects on health
organic chemicals pesticides polychlorinated biphenyls petroleum wastes detergents	agricultural use spillages industrial sewage	effects on health environmental damage destruction of wildlife eutrophication
inorganic chemicals trace elements acids bases	industry leaching of refuse dumps	effects on health reduction in water quality destruction of aquatic life
sediments	leaching wind	reduction in water quality destruction of wildlife
radionuclides	nuclear power stations waste disposal mining	effects on health
thermal	power stations	destruction of aquatic life

4.2 Electrophilic addition.

4.3 Too many nutrients in lakes and rivers, particularly phosphate and nitrate, cause excessive growth of algae and plants. When these plants die and decompose they use up dissolved oxygen from the water. Eventually the oxygen supply becomes so low that fish and other aquatic animals die. The decomposed remains from the algae give off foul-smelling substances.

4.4 Release of nitrate and phosphate to river-water can cause eutrophication.

Chapter 5

5.1 See *figure*.

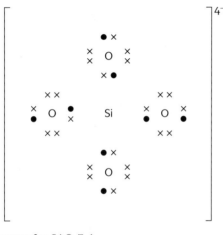

● **Answer for** SAQ 5.1

5.2 The aluminium ion, Al^{3+}, has a high charge density. It neutralises the negative charges on the surfaces of the layers of clay particles, and this breaks up the layer structure to form a precipitate.

5.3 The soil is classified as clay loam. It requires 80 tonnes of lime per hectare.

Chapter 6

6.1 *Figure 6.3* shows that at 3 metres from the road edge lead concentration is $1200\,\mu g$ per g soil in the top 2 cm. This falls to $780\,\mu g$ at a depth of 2–4 cm and to $380\,\mu g$ at a depth of 8–10 cm. The reason for this is that lead is adsorbed on to the surface of clays, which have a large surface area and negative charge. Lead is also held by complexing with organic acids in humus to form a lead-humic acid complex. This restricts the lead from being leached to lower levels.

6.2 The aqueous mixture to be separated is agitated with an organic solvent that is immiscible with water. The constituents dissolve in different quantities in the organic solvent and in the aqueous solution. Repeated extraction with fresh solvent leads to separation of the mixture.

Index (Numbers in italics refer to figures.)